# Co...

# Alberta
# BIRDS

*Contributors:*

*John Acorn, Chris Fisher, Andy Bezener,*

*Gregory Kennedy, Krista Kagume & Carmen Adams*

Lone Pine Publishing

© 2005 by Lone Pine Publishing
First printed in 2005   10 9 8 7 6 5 4 3 2
Printed in China

**The Publisher: Lone Pine Publishing**
10145 – 81 Avenue
Edmonton, AB  T6E 1W9

**Website:** www.lonepinepublishing.com

**Library and Archives Canada Cataloguing in Publication**

Compact guide to Alberta birds / contributors, John Acorn ... [et al.].

Includes bibliographical references and index.
ISBN-13: 978-1-55105-469-8.--ISBN-10: 1-55105-469-8

1. Birds--Alberta--Identification.  2. Bird watching--Alberta. I. Acorn, John, 1958-

QL685.5.A86C64 2005        598'.097123        C2004-907254-4

*Editorial Director:* Nancy Foulds
*Project Editor:* Carmen Adams
*Production Manager:* Gene Longson
*Book Design:* Curt Pillipow
*Cover Design:* Gerry Dotto
*Cover Illustration:* Gary Ross
*Illustrations:* Gary Ross, Ted Nordhagen, Ewa Pluciennik
*Egg Photography:* Alan Bibby
*Layout & Production:* Elliot Engley
*Scanning & Digital Film:* Elite Lithographers Co.

We acknowledge the financial support of the Government of Canada through the Book Publishing Industry Development Program (BPIDP) for our publishing activities.

PC: 14

# Contents

**WATERFOWL**

Snow Goose
size 107 cm • p. 18

Canada Goose
size 107 cm • p. 20

Tundra Swan
size 135 cm • p. 22

Mallard
size 61 cm • p. 24

Northern Pintail
size 63 cm • p. 26

Bufflehead
size 36 cm • p. 28

**GROUSE & PHEASANTS**

Ring-necked Pheasant
size 43 cm • p. 30

Ruffed Grouse
size 43 cm • p. 32

Common Loon
size 80 cm • p. 34

**DIVING BIRDS**

Red-necked Grebe
size 50 cm • p. 36

American White Pelican
size 160 cm • p. 38

Double-crested Cormorant
size 74 cm • p. 40

**BITTERNS, HERONS & VULTURES**

American Bittern
size 64 cm • p. 42

Great Blue Heron
size 135 cm • p. 44

Turkey Vulture
size 72 cm • p. 46

**BIRDS OF PREY**

Bald Eagle
size 93 cm • p. 48

Northern Harrier
size 51 cm • p. 50

Sharp-shinned Hawk
size 33 cm • p. 52

**Red-tailed Hawk**
size 57 cm • p. 54

**Peregrine Falcon**
size 43 cm • p. 56

**Sora**
size 23 cm • p. 58

**American Coot**
size 115 cm • p. 60

**Sandhill Crane**
size 115 cm • p. 62

**Killdeer**
size 26 cm • p. 64

**Lesser Yellowlegs**
size 27 cm • p. 66

**Spotted Sandpiper**
size 19 cm • p. 68

**Wilson's Snipe**
size 28 cm • p. 70

**Wilson's Phalarope**
size 23 cm • p. 72

**Franklin's Gull**
size 49 cm • p. 74

**Ring-billed Gull**
size 49 cm • p. 76

**Common Tern**
size 37 cm • p. 78

**Black Tern**
size 24 cm • p. 80

**Rock Pigeon**
size 32 cm • p. 82

**Mourning Dove**
size 31 cm • p. 84

**Great Horned Owl**
size 55 cm • p. 86

**Snowy Owl**
size 60 cm • p. 88

**OWLS**

Burrowing Owl
size 21 cm • p. 90

Northern Saw-whet Owl
size 21 cm • p. 92

Common Nighthawk
size 24 cm • p. 94

**NIGHTHAWKS & HUMMINGBIRDS**

Ruby-throated Hummingbird
size 9 cm • p. 96

Belted Kingfisher
size 32 cm • p. 98

Downy Woodpecker
size 17 cm • p. 100

**WOODPECKERS & FLICKERS**

Northern Flicker
size 33 cm • p. 102

Pileated Woodpecker
size 45 cm • p. 104

Least Flycatcher
size 19 cm • p. 106

**FLYCATCHERS & KINGBIRDS**

Eastern Kingbird
size 22 cm • p. 108

Northern Shrike
size 25 cm • p. 110

Red-eyed Vireo
size 15 cm • p. 112

**SHRIKES & VIREOS**

Gray Jay
size 31 cm • p. 114

Blue Jay
size 30 cm • p. 116

Black-billed Magpie
size 30 cm • p. 118

**JAYS, CROWS & RAVENS**

American Crow
size 48 cm • p. 120

Common Raven
size 61 cm • p. 122

Horned Lark
size 18 cm • p. 124

LARKS & SWALLOWS

Tree Swallow
size 19 cm • p. 126

Barn Swallow
size 18 cm • p. 128

Black-capped Chickadee
size 14 cm • p. 130

CHICKADEES, WRENS & NUTHATCHES

Red-breasted Nuthatch
size 11 cm • p. 132

Brown Creeper
size 13 cm • p. 134

House Wren
size 12 cm • p. 136

KINGLETS, BLUEBIRDS & ROBINS

Ruby-crowned Kinglet
size 10 cm • p. 138

Mountain Bluebird
size 18 cm • p. 140

American Robin
size 25 cm • p. 142

MIMICS, STARLINGS & WAXWINGS

Gray Catbird
size 23 cm • p. 144

Brown Thrasher
size 22 cm • p. 146

European Starling
size 22 cm • p. 148

WOOD-WARBLERS & TANAGERS

Cedar Waxwing
size 18 cm • p. 150

Yellow Warbler
size 13 cm • p. 152

Common Yellowthroat
size 13 cm • p. 154

SPARROWS

Western Tanager
size 18 cm • p. 156

Chipping Sparrow
size 14 cm • p. 158

Song Sparrow
size 16 cm • p. 160

**JUNCOS & GROSBEAKS**

Dark-eyed Junco
size 16 cm • p. 162

Rose-breasted Grosbeak
size 21 cm • p. 164

Red-winged Blackbird
size 21 cm • p. 166

**BLACKBIRDS & ALLIES**

Western Meadowlark
size 24 cm • p. 168

Yellow-headed Blackbird
size 21 cm • p. 170

Brown-headed Cowbird
size 17 cm • p. 172

Baltimore Oriole
size 19 cm • p. 174

Purple Finch
size 14 cm • p. 176

White-winged Crossbill
size 14 cm • p. 178

**FINCHLIKE BIRDS**

Common Redpoll
size 13 cm • p. 180

House Sparrow
size 16 cm • p. 182

# Introduction

If you have ever admired a songbird's pleasant notes, been fascinated by a soaring hawk or wondered how woodpeckers keep sawdust out of their nostrils, this book is for you. There is so much to discover about birds and their surroundings that birding is becoming one of the fastest growing hobbies. Many people find it relaxing, while others enjoy its outdoor appeal. Some people see it as a way to reconnect with nature, an opportunity to socialize with like-minded people or a way to monitor the environment.

Whether you are just beginning to take an interest in birds or can already identify many species, there is always more to learn. We've highlighted both the remarkable traits and the more typical behaviours displayed by some of Alberta's most abundant and noteworthy birds. A few live in specialized habitats, but most are common species that you have a good chance of encountering in your backyard or on a birdwatching outing.

## BIRDING IN ALBERTA

Almost 400 bird species are found in Alberta on a regular basis, largely because of the geographical and biological diversity of the province. Burrowing Owls survey the southern grasslands, colourful warblers flit through the vast northern forests and boisterous magpies show up just about everywhere. Some species, such as jays, chickadees

Bufflehead

and finches, can be seen year-round. Many others visit Alberta to breed or pass through during annual migrations between arctic nesting grounds and southern wintering areas. Though it is hard to believe that our harsh winters could be inviting to any creature, a few birds, such as the Snowy Owl, are found in our area only in the winter.

Identifying birds in action and under varying conditions involves skill, timing and luck. The more you know about a bird—its range, preferred habitat, food preferences and hours and seasons of activity—the better your chances will be of finding it. Generally, spring and fall are the busiest birding times. Temperatures are moderate, many species of birds are on the move and male songbirds are belting out their unique courtship songs. Birds are usually most active in the early morning hours, except in winter when they are more likely to forage during the milder temperatures of mid-day.

Another useful clue for correctly recognizing birds is knowledge of their habitat. Simply put, a bird's habitat is the place where it normally lives. Some birds prefer open water, some birds are found in cattail marshes, others like mature coniferous forest, and still others prefer abandoned agricultural fields overgrown with tall grass and shrubs. Habitats are just like neighbourhoods: if you associate friends with the suburb in which they live, you can easily learn to associate specific birds with their preferred habitats.

*American Robin*

Only in migration, especially during inclement weather, do some birds leave their usual habitat.

Alberta has a long tradition of friendly, recreational birding. In general, Alberta birders are willing to share their knowledge and involve novices in their projects. Christmas bird counts, breeding bird surveys, nest box programs, migration monitoring and birding lectures and workshops provide a chance for birdwatchers of all levels to interact and share the splendour of birds. Bird hotlines in Alberta provide up-to-date information on the sightings of rarities, which are often easier to locate than you might think. For more information or to participate in these projects, contact the following organizations:

**Federation of Alberta Naturalists**
11759 Groat Road
Edmonton, Alberta T5M 3K6
Phone: (780) 427-8124
Web: http://www.fanweb.ca

**Calgary Area Outdoor Council**
1111 Memorial Drive NW
Calgary, Alberta T2N 3E4
Phone: (403) 270-2262
Web: http://www.caoc.ab.ca

*American White Pelican*

**Canadian Nature Federation**
Suite 606, 1 Nicholas Street
Ottawa, Ontario K1N 7B7
Phone: (613) 562-3447
Web: http://www.cnf.ca

**Bird Hotlines**
Calgary: (403) 237-8821
Northern and Central Alberta: (780) 433-BIRD (2473)

## BIRD FEEDING

Many people set up bird feeders in their backyards, especially in winter. It is possible to attract specific birds by choosing the right kind of food and style of feeder. Keep your feeder stocked through late spring, because birds have a hard time finding food before the flowers bloom and insects hatch. Contrary to popular opinion, birds do not become dependent on feeders, nor do they subsequently forget to forage naturally. Be sure to clean your feeder and the surrounding area regularly to prevent the spread of disease.

Landscaping your property with native plants is another way of providing natural foods for birds. Flocks of waxwings have a keen eye for red mountain ash berries and hummingbirds enjoy columbine flowers. The cumulative effects of "nature-scaping" urban yards can be a significant step toward habitat conservation (especially when you consider that habitat is often lost in small amounts—a seismic line is cut in one area and a highway is built in another). Many good books and web sites about attracting wildlife to your backyard are available.

## ABOUT THE SPECIES ACCOUNTS

This book gives detailed accounts of 83 species of birds that can be expected in Alberta on an annual basis. The order of the birds and their common and scientific names follows the American Ornithologists' Union's *Check-list of North American Birds* (7th ed.) and its supplements.

As well as showing the identifying features of the bird, each species account also attempts to bring the bird to life by describing its various character traits. One of the challenges of birding is that many species look different in spring and summer than they do in fall and winter. Many birds have breeding and nonbreeding plumages, and immature birds often look different from their parents. This book does not describe or illustrate all the different plumages of a species; instead, its focus is on the forms that are most likely to be seen in our area.

**ID** and **Other ID:** Large illustrations point out prominent field marks that will help you to identify each bird. Common, easily understood terms are used for the descriptions, rather than technical terms. Some of the most common anatomical features of birds are pointed out in the glossary illustration (p. 185).

**Size:** The average length of the bird's body from bill to tail, as well as wingspan, are given and are approximate measurements of the bird as it is seen in nature. The size is sometimes given as a range, because there is variation between individuals, or between males and females.

**Voice:** You will hear many birds, particularly songbirds, which may remain hidden from view. Memorable paraphrases of distinctive sounds will aid you in identifying a species by ear.

**Status:** A general comment, such as "common," "uncommon" or "rare," is usually sufficient to describe the relative abundance of a species. Situations are bound to vary somewhat since migratory pulses, seasonal changes and centres of activity tend to concentrate or disperse birds.

**Habitat:** The habitats listed describe where each species is most commonly found. In most cases, it is a general description unless the bird is restricted to a specific habitat.

Birds can turn up in almost any type of habitat, but they will usually be found in environments that provide the specific food, water, cover and, in some cases, nesting habitat that they need to survive.

**Similar Birds:** Easily confused species are illustrated for each account. If you concentrate on the most relevant field marks, the subtle differences between species can be reduced to easily identifiable traits. Remember, even experienced birders can mistake one species for another. Some of the similar birds shown are accidental species and very rarely seen in the province.

**Nesting:** In each species account, a photo of the bird's egg is provided and nest location and structure, clutch size, incubation period and parental duties are discussed. Remember that birding ethics discourage the disturbance of active bird nests. If a nest is disturbed, you may drive away the parents during a critical period or expose defenceless young to predators. Because bird egg colours vary, egg colour descriptions may not always match the photo.

*Common Raven*

**Range Maps:** The range map for each species shows the overall range of the species in an average year. Most birds will confine their annual movements to this range, although each year some birds wander beyond their traditional boundaries. The maps show breeding, summer and winter ranges, as well as migratory pathways—areas of the region where birds may appear while en route to nesting or winter habitat. The representations of the pathways do not distinguish high-use migration corridors from areas that are seldom used.

## Range Map Symbols

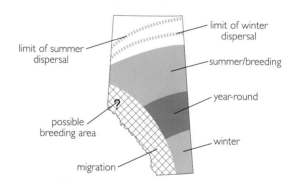

limit of summer dispersal

limit of winter dispersal

summer/breeding

year-round

possible breeding area

winter

migration

*Northern Flicker*

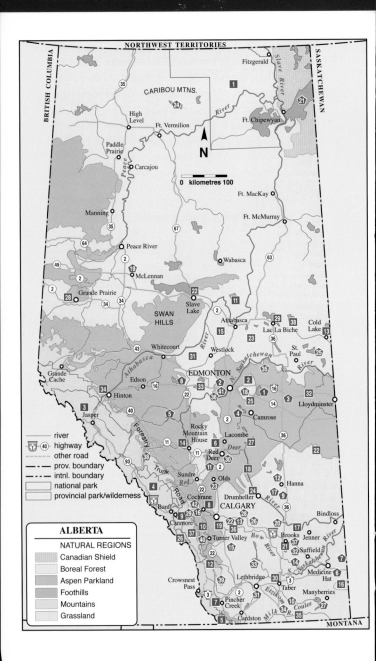

**ALBERTA**

NATURAL REGIONS
- Canadian Shield
- Boreal Forest
- Aspen Parkland
- Foothills
- Mountains
- Grassland

river
highway
other road
prov. boundary
intnl. boundary
national park
provincial park/wilderness

**NATIONAL PARKS**
1 Wood Buffalo NP
2 Elk Island NP
3 Jasper NP
4 Banff NP
5 Waterton Lakes NP

**PROVINCIAL PARKS**
6 Aspen Beach PP
7 Beauvais Lake PP
8 Big Hill Springs PP
9 Bow Valley PP
10 Brown-Lowery PP
11 Calling Lake PP
12 Chain Lakes PP

13 Cold Lake PP
14 Crimson Lake PP
15 Cross Lake PP
16 Cypress Hills PP
17 Dinosaur PP
18 Dry Island Buffalo Jump PP
19 Fish Creek PP
20 Gooseberry Lake PP
21 Kinbrook Island PP
22 Lesser Slave Lake PP
23 Long Lake PP
24 Midland PP
25 Miquelon Lakes PP
26 Peter Lougheed PP
27 Rochon Sands PP

28 Saskatoon Island PP
29 Sir Winston Churchill PP
30 Taber PP
31 Thunder Lake PP
32 Vermilion PP
33 Wabamun Lake PP
34 William A. Switzer PP
35 Writing-on-Stone PP
36 Wyndham-Carseland PP

**OTHER**
37 Kananaskis Country
38 Lakeland Provincial
     Recreation Area

**LAKES & RESERVOIRS**
1 Beaverhill Lake
2 Big Lake
3 Birch Lake
4 Bittern Lake
5 Brazeau Reservoir
6 Cavan Lake
7 Chappice Lake
8 Chip Lake
9 Coleman Lake
10 Crow Indian Lake
11 Dickson Dam
12 Dowling Lake
13 Eagle Lake
14 Fincastle Lake
15 Frank Lake

16 Ghost Dam
17 Handhills Lake
18 Hastings Lake
19 Kimiwan Lake
20 Kitsim Reservoir
21 Lake Athabasca
22 Langdon Reservoir
23 Lost Lake
24 Margaret Lake
25 Muriel Lake
26 Namaka Lake
27 Pakowki Lake
28 Scope Lake
29 Seebe Dam
30 Slack Slough
31 Stirling Lake

32 Tilley Reservoir
33 Travers Reservoir
34 Verdigris Lake
35 Whitford Lake

**OTHER BIRDING SITES**
36 Clifford E. Lee
     Nature Sanctuary
37 Kininvie Marsh
38 Kootenay Plains
39 Porcupine Hills
40 Sheep River
     Wildlife Sanctuary
41 Wagner Natural Area
42 Wildcat Hills

## ALBERTA'S TOP BIRDING SITES

Alberta is as diverse as it is large, with arid grasslands, rustling aspen forests and majestic Rocky Mountains. Our province can be separated into six natural regions: Canadian Shield, Boreal Forest, Aspen Parkland, Foothills, Mountains and Grassland. Each region is composed of a number of different habitats that support a wealth of wildlife.

There are hundreds of good birding areas throughout the province. The areas indicated on the map have been selected to represent a broad range of bird communities and habitats, with an emphasis on accessibility.

# Snow Goose
*Chen caerulescens*

Noisy flocks of Snow Geese can be quite entertaining, creating a moving patchwork in the sky with their black wing tips and white plumage. • These geese breed in the Arctic and northeastern Siberia, crossing the Bering Strait twice a year. Their smiling, serrated bills are made for grazing on short arctic tundra and gripping the slippery roots of marsh plants. • Snow Geese are strong walkers as well as flyers. They have been known to travel up to 75 kilometres on foot in search of suitable habitat and fly at speeds up to 35 kilometres per hour.

**Other ID:** plumage is occasionally stained rusty red; pink feet and bill. *Blue morph:* white head and upper neck; dark blue grey body. *In flight:* black wing tips.
**Size:** L 71–84 cm; W 1.4–1.5 m.
**Voice:** loud, nasal, *houk-houk* in flight, higher pitched and more constant than Canada Goose.
**Status:** locally common migrant.
**Habitat:** croplands, fields, open areas, lakes and ponds.

## Similar Birds

Ross's Goose     Tundra Swan (p. 22)     Trumpeter Swan     Mute Swan

blue morph

dark "grin" on bill

white overall

**Nesting:** does not nest in Alberta; female builds nest lined with grass, feathers and down, in a hollow on the ground; creamy white eggs are 79 x 52 mm; female incubates 4–7 eggs for 22–25 days.

## Did You Know?

The Snow Goose has two colour morphs—white and blue—which, until 1983, were considered two different species.

## Look For

Snow Geese fly in wavy, disorganized lines, versus the V-formation of Canada Geese. Occasionally they migrate together in mixed flocks.

# Canada Goose
*Branta canadensis*

Canada Geese mate for life and are devoted parents. Unlike most birds, the family stays together for nearly a year, which helps to increase the survival rate of the young. • Wild geese can be aggressive, especially when defending young or competing for food. Hissing sounds and low, outstretched necks are signs that you should give these birds some space. • Geese graze on aquatic grasses and sprouts and you may spot them tipping up to grab aquatic roots and tubers. • Recently, the smaller Canada Goose that breeds in Alaska, Yukon and the Northwest Territories, and winters mostly along the coast, became its own species named the "Cackling Goose."

**Other ID:** light brown underparts; dark brown upperparts.
**Size:** *L* 55–122 cm; *W* up to 1.8 m.
**Voice:** loud, familiar *ah-honk*.
**Status:** common migrant and breeder; a few overwinter.
**Habitat:** lakeshores, riverbanks, ponds, farmlands and city parks.

## Similar Birds

Brant

Greater White-fronted Goose

Snow Goose (p. 18)

long, black neck

white "chin strap"

short, black tail

white undertail coverts

**Nesting:** usually on the ground; female builds a nest of grasses and mud, lined with down; white eggs are 87 x 58 mm; female incubates 3–8 eggs for 25–28 days; goslings are born in May.

## Did You Know?

A migrating Canada Goose will occasionally allow a smaller bird to hitch a ride on a its back!

## Look For

Big flocks of Canada Geese return to Alberta in April, and the first downy goslings of the year are normally seen before mid-May.

# Tundra Swan
*Cygnus columbianus*

A wave of Tundra Swans flying overhead is a sight you will never forget. They pass through our province in April, usually reaching their arctic breeding grounds before the spring thaw. In October, you can spot them again, this time heading south. • The windpipe of the Tundra Swan loops through the bird's sternum, which amplifies its call. In Europe, this bird is called the "Whistling Swan."

**Other ID:** slightly concave bill; black feet.
**Size:** L 1.2–1.5 m; W 2 m.
**Voice:** high-pitched, quivering *oo-oo-whoo* repeated-in flight.
**Status:** common migrant.
**Habitat:** staging areas include shallow areas of lakes and wetlands, agricultural fields and flooded pastures.

## Similar Birds

Trumpeter Swan          Mute Swan          Snow Goose (p. 18)

yellow lores

neck is held
straight up

large, black bill

white plumage

**Nesting:** does not nest in Alberta; nest is
a large mound of vegetation; creamy white
eggs are 107 x 68 mm; female usually incubates
4–5 eggs for 31–32 days.

## Did You Know?

Tundra Swans take over
three months to migrate
from the Atlantic to
the Arctic, but the
swans spend only about
114 hours in the air.

## Look For

A good time to visit a staging
area is in the evening when
swans stop to rest and refuel
on waste grain and aquatic
vegetation in Alberta's fields
and wetlands.

# Mallard
## *Anas platyrhynchos*

The male Mallard, with his shiny green head and chestnut brown breast, is the classic wild duck. Mallards can be seen year-round, often in flocks and always near open water. These confident ducks have even been spotted dabbling in outdoor swimming pools. • Most people think the Mallard's quack is the typical duck call, but this bird is one of only a few ducks that really "quacks." The croak of a male wood frog sounds suspiciously similar to a Mallard's call, so don't be fooled in early spring.

**Other ID:** orange feet. *Male:* white "necklace"; black tail feathers curl upward. *In flight:* dark blue speculum bordered by white.
**Size:** *L* 51–71 cm; *W* 89 cm.
**Voice:** quacks; female is louder than male.
**Status:** very common migrant and breeder; many overwinter on open water.
**Habitat:** lakes, wetlands, rivers, city parks, agricultural areas and sewage lagoons.

## Similar Birds

Northern Shoveler

American Black Duck

Common Merganser

glossy, green head

orange bill is spattered with black

yellow bill

chestnut brown breast

mottled brown overall

**Nesting:** grass nest is built on the ground or under a bush; creamy, grayish or greenish white eggs are 58 x 41 mm; female incubates 7–10 eggs for 26–30 days.

## Did You Know?

A nesting hen generates enough body heat to make the grasses around her nest grow faster. She uses the tall grasses to further conceal her precious nest.

## Look For

After breeding, male ducks lose their elaborate plumage, helping them stay camouflaged during their flightless period. In early fall, they molt back into breeding colours.

# Northern Pintail
*Anas acuta*

A long neck and a long, tapered tail put this dabbling duck in a class of its own. The elegant and graceful Northern Pintail is not unique to North America; it also breeds in Asia and Northern Europe. • These migrants arrive early to scout out flooded agricultural fields for choice nesting locations. Unfortunately, Northern Pintails usually build their nests in vulnerable areas, on exposed ground near water, which has resulted in a slow decline in their population. Recent efforts at staging and feeding habitat management, as well as harvesting restrictions, are helping to stabilize their numbers.

**Other ID:** *Male:* long, tapering tail feathers; white on breast extends up sides of neck; black-and-white hindquarters.
**Size:** *Male:* L 64–76 cm. *Female:* L 51–56 cm.
**Voice:** *Male:* soft, whistling call. *Female:* rough quack.
**Status:** common migrant and breeder.
**Habitat:** shallow wetlands, fields and lake edges.

## Similar Birds

Mallard (p. 24)

Gadwall

Blue-winged Teal

chocolate
brown head

mottled, light
brown overall

dark,
glossy bill

long,
slender
neck

♂

♀

dusty grey
body plumage

**Nesting:** in a small depression in vegetation; nest of grass, leaves and moss is lined with down; greenish buff eggs are 54 x 37 mm; female incubates 6–12 eggs for 22–25 days.

## Did You Know?

In fall, Northern Pintails gather at marshes and reservoirs, but fly many kilometres to outlying areas to feed, usually at dusk.

## Look For

The long, pointed tail of the male Northern Pintail is easy to see in flight and it points skyward when the Pintail tips up to dabble.

# Bufflehead
*Bucephala albeola*

The tiny Bufflehead might be the first diving duck you learn to identify. With its simple, bold plumage, this abundant duck resembles few other species. • Diving ducks' legs are set near the back of their bodies, so they must run along the surface of the water to gain momentum to take flight. • Buffleheads often nest in tree cavities, using abandoned woodpecker nests or natural holes. After hatching, the ducklings remain in the nest chamber for up to three days before jumping out and tumbling to the ground.

**Other ID:** very small, rounded duck; short neck.
*Male:* white neck and underparts; dark back.
*Female:* dark brown head; light brown sides.
*In-flight:* white speculum on male.
**Size:** L 33–38 cm; W 53 cm.
**Voice:** *Male:* growling call. *Female:* harsh quack.
**Status:** uncommon to common migrant and breeder.
**Habitat:** open water on lakes, large ponds and rivers.

## Similar Birds

Hooded Merganser

Barrow's Goldeneye

Common Goldeneye

white, oval
ear patch

white wedge
on back
of head

iridescent dark green
or purple head usually
appears black

short,
grey bill

**Nesting:** in a tree cavity, often near water;
pale-buff to cream eggs are 51 x 37 mm; female
incubates 6–12 eggs for 28–33 days.

## Did You Know?

The mature female Buffle-
head returns to the area
of her birth to search for
a cavity in which to nest.
These ducks can squeeze
into holes only 8 cm wide!

## Look For

The striking white patch on
the rear of the male's head
stands out, even at a distance.

# Ring-necked Pheasant

*Phasianus colchicus*

Despite the Ring-necked Pheasant's good looks, this introduced Asian bird has many pressures to endure. It was brought to North America in the late 1800s, mainly as a gamebird. Since then, its numbers have had to be continually replenished by hatchery-raised young, not only because they are hunted, but because of diminished habitat, intensive farming practices and harsh winters. • Unlike native grouse, the Ring-necked Pheasant does not have feathered legs and feet for insulation and it cannot live on native plants alone; it depends on grain and corn crops for survival in our area.

**Other ID:** *Male:* bronze underparts. *Female:* mottled brown overall; light underparts.
**Size:** *Male:* L 76–91 cm; W 78 cm.
*Female:*-L-51–66-cm; W 70 cm.
**Voice:** *Male:* loud, raspy, roosterlike crowing: *ka-squawk;* whirring of the wings mostly just before sunrise.
**Status:** uncommon to common year-round resident.
**Habitat:** shrubby grasslands, hayfields, grassy ditches and fencelines, woodlots and occasionally croplands.

## Similar Birds

Ruffed Grouse (p. 32)

Spruce Grouse

naked, red
face patch

green head

white "collar"

large, long,
barred tail

♂

**Nesting:** on the ground, among vegetation or next to a log or other natural debris; in a slight depression lined with grass and leaves; olive buff eggs are 46 x 36 mm; female incubates 10–12 eggs for 23–28 days.

## Did You Know?

The Ring-necked Pheasant does not fly long distances; it exhibits bursts of laboured flight that allows it to escape most predators.

## Look For

The female Ring-necked Pheasant, easily confused with the Ruffed Grouse, has a longer, narrower and more pointed tail, without any broad, dark bands at the tip.

# Ruffed Grouse
*Bonasa umbellus*

If you hear a loud "boom" echoing through the forest, you are likely hearing a Ruffed Grouse "drumming" to announce his territory. Every spring, and occasionally in fall, the male grouse struts along a fallen log with his tail fanned and his neck feathers ruffed, beating the air periodically with accelerating wing-strokes. • In winter, scales grow out along the sides of the Ruffed Grouse's feet, creating temporary "snowshoes." Though many birds can walk on snow, only grouse and ptarmigan have this specialized feature.

**Other ID:** black feathers on sides of lower neck (visible when fluffed out in courtship displays); grey- or reddish barred tail. *Female:* incomplete subterminal tail band.
**Size:** *L* 38–48 cm; *W* 56 cm.
**Voice:** courting male drums to produce deep, accelerating booms.
**Status:** common year-round resident.
**Habitat:** deciduous and mixed forests and riparian woodlands; favours young, second-growth stands with birch and poplar.

## Similar Birds

Spruce Grouse

Sharp-tailed Grouse

small, pointed head crest

mottled,
grey brown
overall

tail has broad,
dark, subterminal
band and white tip

♂ *grey morph*

**Nesting:** in a shallow depression, often beside boulders or under a log; buff-coloured eggs, often with light spotting, are 40 x 30 mm; female incubates 9–12 eggs for 23–25 days.

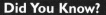

## Did You Know?

During winter, Ruffed Grouse bury themselves in snowbanks to keep warm.

## Look For

As a potential threat approaches, Ruffed Grouse often stand still to camouflage themselves against the forest floor. For every grouse seen, many more go unnoticed.

# Common Loon
*Gavia immer*

When the haunting call of the Common Loon pierces a still evening, cottagers know that summer has begun. Loons actually have several different calls. Frightened loons give a laughing distress call, separated pairs seem to wail *where aaare you?* and groups give soft, cohesive hoots as they fly.

• Common Loons are well suited to their aquatic lifestyle. Most birds have hollow bones, but loons have solid bones that reduce their buoyancy and make diving easier.

**Other ID:** *Nonbreeding:* much duller plumage; sandy brown back; light underparts. *In flight:* long wings beat constantly; hunchbacked appearance; legs trail behind tail.
**Size:** L 71–89 cm; W 1.2–1.5 m.
**Voice:** alarm call is a quavering tremolo; also wails, hoots and yodels.
**Status:** uncommon to common migrant and breeder.
**Habitat:** large lakes, often with islands that provide undisturbed shorelines for nesting.

## Similar Birds

Red-throated Loon          Pacific Loon

*nonbreeding*

green
black head

red eyes

black-and-white
"checkerboard"
upperparts

white
"necklace"

stout, thick,
black bill

*breeding*

♂

white breast
and underparts

**Nesting:** on a muskrat lodge, small island or
shoreline; nest is a mound of aquatic vegetation;
darkly spotted, olive brown eggs are 90 x 57 mm;
both parents incubate 1–3 eggs for 24–31 days
and raise young.

### Did You Know?

Hungry loons will
chase fish to depths of
55 metres—as deep as an
Olympic-sized swimming
pool is long!

### Look For

Rear-placed legs make
walking on land awkward
for these birds.

# Red-necked Grebe
*Podiceps grisegena*

*nonbreeding*

As evening settles over a wetland, the laughing calls of courting Red-necked Grebes signal the beginning of a new spring breeding season. Although Red-necked Grebes are not as vocally refined as loons, few loons can match the energy of a pair of grebes. In late May, their wild laughter often lasts through the night. • Grebes have individually webbed, or "lobed," feet. The three forward-facing toes have special flanges that are not connected to the other toes. • These birds feed, sleep and court on water.

**Other ID:** black upperparts; light underparts; dark eyes. *Nonbreeding:* greyish white foreneck, "chin" and "cheek."
**Size:** *L* 43–56 cm; *W* 61 cm.
**Voice:** often-repeated, laughlike, excited *ah-ooo ah-ooo ah-ooo ah-ah-ah-ah-ah.*
**Status:** uncommon to locally common migrant and breeder.
**Habitat:** open, deep lakes.

## Similar Birds

Horned Grebe

Pied-billed Grebe

Eared Grebe

black crown

whitish "cheek"

rusty neck

straight, heavy bill is dark above and yellow underneath

*breeding*

**Nesting:** usually singly or in loose colonies; floating platform nest is anchored to pondweeds; white eggs, often stained by vegetation, are 56 x 36 mm; both parents incubate 4–5 eggs for 20–23 days.

## Did You Know?

It is thought that grebes eat feathers to line their digestive tracts, protecting their organs from sharp fish bones or parasites.

## Look For

Grebes carry their newly hatched, striped young on their backs. The young stay aboard even when the parents dive underwater.

# American White Pelican
*Pelecanus erythrorhynchos*

This majestic wetland bird is one of only a few bird species that feeds cooperatively. A group of pelicans will herd fish into a school, then dip their bucketlike bills into the water to capture their prey. In a single scoop, a pelican can trap over 12 litres of water and fish in its bill, which is about two to three times as much as its stomach can hold. This impressive feat inspired Dixon Lanier Merritt to write: "A wonderful bird is a pelican. His bill holds more than his belican!"

short tail

**Other ID:** very large, stocky white bird; black primary and secondary wing feathers. *Breeding*: small, keeled plate develops on upper mandible; pale yellow crest on back of head.
**Size:** *L* 1.4–1.8 m; *W* 2.8 m.
**Voice:** generally quiet; rarely issues piglike grunts.
**Status:** uncommon to locally common migrant and breeder.
**Habitat:** large lakes or rivers.

## Similar Birds

Tundra Swan (p. 22)          Trumpeter Swan          Mute Swan

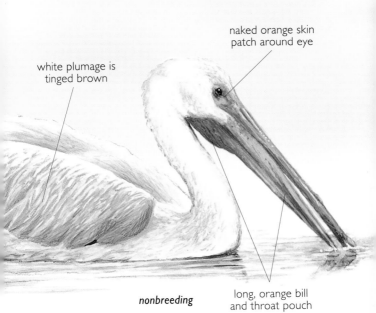

white plumage is
tinged brown

naked orange skin
patch around eye

*nonbreeding*

long, orange bill
and throat pouch

**Nesting:** colonial; on a bare, low-lying island;
scrape nest is unlined or lined with debris;
dull white eggs, often with some streaking
or discoloration, are 87 x 56 mm; pair incubates
2 eggs for 29–36 days.

## Did You Know?

The feathers on a pelican's
wing tips are black and
have a pigment called
melanin that doesn't wear
in the wind.

## Look For

When pelicans fly into the
wind, they often stay close to
the surface of the water.
When the wind is at their
backs, they fly much higher.

# Double-crested Cormorant

*Phalacrocorax auritus*

The Double-crested Cormorant looks like a bird but smells and swims like a fish. With a long, rudderlike tail and excellent underwater vision, this slick-feathered bird has mastered the underwater world. Most water birds have waterproof feathers, but the structure of the Double-crested Cormorant's unique feathers allows water in, making this bird less buoyant and a better diver. The Double-crested Cormorant also has sealed nostrils for diving, and, therefore, must fly with its bill open to breathe.

**Other ID:** blue eyes. *Breeding:* throat pouch becomes intense orange yellow. *In flight:* rapid wingbeats; kinked neck.
**Size:** *L* 66–81 cm; *W* 1.3 m.
**Voice:** generally quiet; may issue piglike grunts or croaks, especially near nest colonies.
**Status:** uncommon to locally common migrant and breeder.
**Habitat:** large lakes and large, meandering rivers.

## Similar Birds

Canada Goose (p. 20)

Common Loon (p. 34)

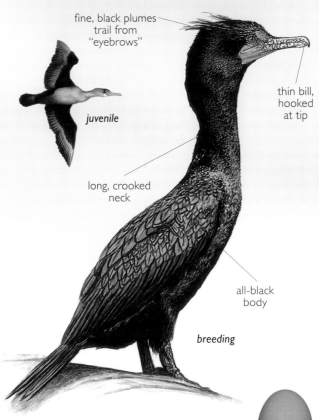

fine, black plumes trail from "eyebrows"

thin bill, hooked at tip

*juvenile*

long, crooked neck

all-black body

*breeding*

**Nesting:** colonial; on an island or high in a tree; platform nest is made of sticks and guano; bluish white eggs are 51 x 38 mm; both sexes incubate 2–7 eggs for 25–30 days.

## Did You Know?

Japanese fishermen sometimes use cormorants on leashes to catch fish. This traditional method of fishing is called *Ukai*.

## Look For

Double-crested Cormorants lack oil glands and will often perch on trees or piers with their wings partly spread to dry out their feathers in the wind.

# American Bittern
*Botaurus lentiginosus*

The American Bittern's deep, pumping call is as common in a spring marsh as the sound of croaking frogs, but this well-camouflaged bird remains hidden. When an intruder approaches, the bittern freezes with its bill pointed skyward—its vertically streaked, brown plumage blends perfectly with the surrounding marsh. In most cases, intruders simply pass by without ever noticing the bird. An American Bittern will adopt this reedlike position even in an open field, apparently unaware that a lack of cover betrays its presence!

**Other ID:** brown streak from "chin" through breast; brown upperparts; yellow legs and feet; dark streak from bill down neck to shoulder; black outer wings. *In flight:* rich buff flanks and sides.
**Size:** *L* 59–69 cm; *W* 1.1 m.
**Voice:** deep, slow, resonant, repetitive *pomp-er-lunk* or *onk-a-BLONK*; most often heard in the evening or at night.
**Status:** uncommon migrant and breeder.
**Habitat:** productive wetlands and lake edges with tall, dense sedges, bulrushes or cattails.

## Similar Birds

Black-crowned Night-Heron

## Look For

Late mornings and early afternoons are the best times to spot this secretive bird.

dark crown

straight, stout bill

white undertail coverts

short tail

*adult*

**Nesting:** above the waterline in dense vegetation; platform nest is made of sedges and reeds; separate paths often lead to nest; pale olive or buff eggs are 49 x 37 mm; female incubates 3–5 eggs for 24–28 days.

## Did You Know?

American Bitterns, like all herons, have dense patches of specialized downy feathers that crumble into a fine powder when the bird preens. The powder coats and waterproofs other feathers.

# Great Blue Heron
*Ardea herodias*

The long-legged Great Blue Heron has a stealthy, often motionless hunting strategy. It waits for a fish or frog to approach, spears the prey with its bill, then flips its catch into the air and swallows it whole. Herons usually hunt near water, but they also stalk fields and meadows in search of rodents. • Great Blue Herons settle in communal treetop nests called rookeries. Nesting herons are sensitive to human disturbance, so observe this bird's behaviour from a distance.

**Other ID:** *Breeding:* richer colours; plumes streak from crown and throat. *In flight:* legs trail behind body; slow, steady wingbeats.
**Size:** L 1.3–1.4 m; W 1.8 m.
**Voice:** quiet away from the nest; occasional harsh *frahnk frahnk frahnk* during takeoff.
**Status:** common migrant and breeder; a few might overwinter.
**Habitat:** forages along edges of rivers, lakes, marshes, fields and wet meadows.

## Similar Birds

Little Blue Heron

Black-crowned
Night-Heron

Great Egret

blue grey overall

straight,
yellow bill

chestnut
brown thighs

long, curving neck
with black markings
on throat

long,
dark legs

*breeding*

**Nesting:** colonial; adds to stick platform nest annually; nest width can reach 1.2 m; pale bluish green eggs are 64 x 45 mm; pair incubates 4–7 eggs for approximately 28 days.

## Did You Know?

The Great Blue Heron is the tallest of all herons and egrets in North America.

## Look For

In flight, the Great Blue Heron folds its neck back over its shoulders in an S-shape. Similar-looking cranes extend their necks when flying.

# Turkey Vulture
*Cathartes aura*

Turkey Vultures are intelligent, playful and social birds. Groups live and sleep together in large trees, or roosts. Some roost sites are over a century old and have been used by the same family of vultures for several generations. • The scientific name *Cathartes aura* means "cleanser" and refers to this bird's affinity for carrion. A vulture's bill and feet are much less powerful than those of eagles, hawks or falcons, which kill live prey. The Turkey Vulture's red, featherless head may appear grotesque, but this adaptation allows the bird to stay relatively clean while feeding on messy carcasses.

**Other ID:** *Immature:* grey head. *In flight:* head appears small; silver grey flight feathers; black wing linings; wings are held in a shallow "V"; rocks from side to side when soaring.
**Size:** *L* 65–80 cm; *W* 1.7–1.8 m.
**Voice:** generally silent; occasionally produces a hiss or grunt if threatened.
**Status:** uncommon migrant and breeder.
**Habitat:** usually flies over open country, shorelines or roads; rarely over forests.

## Similar Birds

Golden Eagle

Bald Eagle (p. 48)

bare, red head

pale, hooked bill

all-black plumage

*adult*

**Nesting:** in a cave, crevice, log or among boulders; uses no nest material; dull white eggs, irregularly marked with brown or purple, are 71 x 49 mm; pair incubates 2 eggs for up to 41 days.

## Did You Know?

No other bird uses updrafts and thermals in flight as well as the Turkey Vulture. Pilots have reported seeing vultures soaring at 6000 m!

## Look For

A threatened Turkey Vulture will either play dead or throw up. The vomit's odour repulses attackers, much like the odour of a skunk's spray.

# Bald Eagle
*Haliaeetus leucocephalus*

Part of the sea eagle group, the majestic Bald Eagle feeds mostly on fish and is often found near water. While soaring hundreds of metres high in the air, an eagle can spot fish swimming underwater and small rodents scurrying through the grass. Eagles

*immature*

also scavenge carrion and steal food from other birds. • Bald Eagles do not mature until their fourth or fifth year—only then will they develop the characteristic white head and tail plumage.

**Other ID:** *1st-year:* dark overall; dark bill; some white in underwings. *2nd-year:* dark "bib"; white in underwings. *3rd-year:* mostly white plumage; yellow at base of bill; yellow eyes. *4th-year:* light head with dark facial streak; variable pale-and-dark plumage; all yellow bill; paler eyes. *In flight:* white tail; broad wings are held flat.
**Size:** *L* 76–109 cm; *W* 1.7–2.4 m.
**Voice:** thin, weak squeal or gull-like cackle: *kleek-kik-kik-kik* or *kah-kah-kah.*
**Status:** uncommon migrant and breeder; some overwinter near open water.
**Habitat:** large lakes and rivers.

## Similar Birds

Golden Eagle

Osprey

white head

yellow bill

yellow feet

*adult*

**Nesting:** in a tree; usually near water; huge stick nest is often reused for many years; white eggs are 71 x 54 mm; pair incubates 1–3 eggs for 34–36 days.

### Did You Know?

Bald Eagles add sticks to their nests to renew pair bonds. Nests can be up to 4.5 m in diameter, the largest of any North American bird.

### Look For

In winter, hundreds of ducks gather on industrial ponds or other ice-free waters, unknowingly providing an easy meal for hungry Bald Eagles.

# Northern Harrier
*Circus cyaneus*

With its prominent white rump and distinctive, slightly upturned wings, the Northern Harrier may be the easiest raptor to identify in flight. Unlike other midsized birds, it often flies close to the ground, relying on sudden surprise attacks to capture prey. • The courtship flight of the Northern Harrier is a spectacle worth watching in the spring. The male climbs almost vertically in the air, then stalls and plummets in a reckless dive toward the ground. At the last second he saves himself with a hairpin turn that sends him skyward again.

**Other ID:** facial disc; white rump. *Male:* blue grey to silver grey upperparts; white underparts; indistinct tail bands, except for 1 dark subterminal band.
*In-flight:* black wing tips.
**Size:** L 41–61 cm; W 1.1–1.2 m.
**Voice:** generally quiet; high-pitched *ke-ke-ke-ke-ke-ke* near the nest or during courtship.
**Status:** common migrant and breeder.
**Habitat:** open country, including fields, wet meadows, cattail marshes, bogs and croplands.

## Similar Birds

Rough-legged Hawk          Red-tailed Hawk (p. 54)

dark brown
upperparts

long, dark-
banded tail

streaky
brown-and-buff
underparts

**Nesting:** on the ground; usually in tall vegetation or on a raised mound; shallow depression is lined with grass, sticks and cattails; bluish white eggs are 47 x 36 mm; female incubates 4–6 eggs for 30–32 days.

## Did You Know?

Britain's Royal Air Force was so impressed by the Northern Harrier's manoeuvrability that it named the Harrier aircraft after this bird.

## Look For

The Northern Harrier's owl-like, parabolic facial disc reflects sound inward, allowing this bird to hunt by sound as well as sight.

# Sharp-shinned Hawk
*Accipiter striatus*

After a successful hunt, the small Sharp-shinned Hawk often perches on a favourite "plucking post" with its meal in its razor-sharp talons. Sharpies are members of the *Accipter* genus, or woodland hawks, and they prey almost exclusively on small birds. Their short, rounded wings, long, rudderlike tails and flap-and-glide flight pattern allow them to manoeuvre through the forest at high speed.
• When delivering food to his nestlings, a male Sharp-shinned Hawk takes care not to disturb his mate—she is typically one-third larger than he is, and notoriously short-tempered.

**Other ID:** red eyes; dark barring on pale under-wings. *In flight:* flap-and-glide flyer; very agile in wooded areas.
**Size:** *Male:* L 25–30 cm; W 51–61 cm. *Female:* L-30–36 cm; W 61–71 cm.
**Voice:** usually silent; intense, repeated *kik-kik-kik-kik* during the breeding season.
**Status:** uncommon migrant and breeder.
**Habitat:** dense to semi-open forests and large woodlots; occasionally along rivers and in urban areas; favours bogs and dense, moist, coniferous forests for nesting.

## Similar Birds

Cooper's Hawk
American Kestrel
Merlin

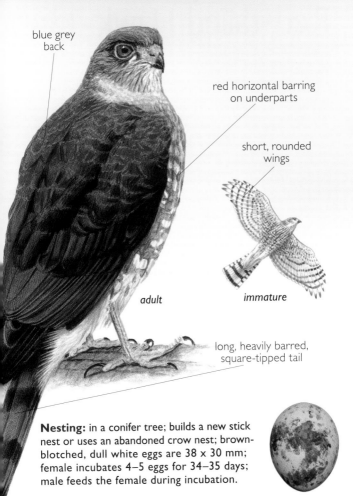

blue grey back

red horizontal barring on underparts

short, rounded wings

*adult*

*immature*

long, heavily barred, square-tipped tail

**Nesting:** in a conifer tree; builds a new stick nest or uses an abandoned crow nest; brown-blotched, dull white eggs are 38 x 30 mm; female incubates 4–5 eggs for 34–35 days; male feeds the female during incubation.

## Did You Know?

As it ages, the Sharp-shinned Hawk's bright yellow eyes become red. This change may signal full-maturity to potential mates.

## Look For

In the winter, watch for Sharp-shinned Hawks visiting your backyard bird feeders to prey on feeding sparrows and finches.

# Red-tailed Hawk

*Buteo jamaicensis*

On an afternoon drive along our province's highways, you might spot a pair of Red-tailed Hawks. The light phase "Krider's Hawk" and the dark-phase "Harlan's Hawk" both live in Alberta and can be difficult to recognize. • In warm weather, the broad wings and tail of this buteo help it to soar on thermals and updrafts. These pockets of rising air provide substantial lift, which allows migrating hawks to fly for almost 3 kilometres without flapping their wings once. On cooler days, resident Red-tails perch on exposed tree limbs, fence posts or utility poles to scan for prey.

**Other ID:** *In flight:* fan-shaped tail; white or occasionally tawny brown underside and underwing linings; dark leading edge on underside of wing; light underwing flight feathers with faint barring.
**Size:** *Male:* L 46–58 cm; W 1.1–1.5 m.
*Female:*-L-51–64 cm; W 1.1–1.5 m.
**Voice:** powerful, descending scream: *keeearrrr!*
**Status:** very common migrant and breeder.
**Habitat:** open country with some trees; also roadsides, fields or woodlots.

## Similar Birds

Rough-legged Hawk

Broad-winged Hawk

Swainson's
Hawk

dark upperparts with some white highlights

dark brown band of streaks across belly

*adult*

red tail

**Nesting:** in woodlands adjacent to open habitat; bulky stick nest is enlarged each year; brown-blotched, whitish eggs are 59 x 47 mm; pair incubates 2–4 eggs for 28–35 days.

## Did You Know?

The Red-tailed Hawk's piercing call is often paired with the image of an eagle in TV commercials and movies.

## Look For

Courting pairs dive at each other, lock talons in the air and tumble toward the earth. They break away at the last second, just before crashing to the ground.

# Peregrine Falcon
*Falco peregrinus*

Nothing causes more panic in a flock of ducks or shorebirds than a hunting Peregrine Falcon. This powerful raptor matches every twist and turn the flock makes, then dives to strike a lethal blow.

• Peregrine Falcons represent a successful conservation effort. In the 1960s, the pesticide DDT caused peregrines to lay eggs with thin, easily breakable shells. Peregrine populations declined dramatically until DDT was banned in North America in 1972. Since then, hundreds of captive-bred peregrines have been successfully reintroduced to the wild.

**Other ID:** *In flight:* pointed wings; long, narrow, dark-banded tail.
**Size:** *Male:* L 38–43 cm; W 94–109 cm.
*Female:*-L-43–48 cm; W 1.1–1.2 m.
**Voice:** loud, harsh, continuous *cack-cack-cack-cack-cack* near the nest site.
**Status:** rare to uncommon migrant and breeder.
**Habitat:** lakeshores, river valleys, river mouths, urban areas and open fields.

## Similar Birds

Gyrfalcon

Merlin

prominent, dark "helmet"

blue grey back

white to buff "chin" and throat

*adult*

yellow feet

light underparts with dark, fine spotting and flecking

**Nesting:** usually on a rocky cliff or cutbank; may use a skyscraper ledge; nest site is often reused and littered with prey remains; white eggs with reddish, brownish or purple blotches are 53 x 41 mm; pair incubates 3–5 eggs for 32–34 days.

## Did You Know?

The Peregrine Falcon is the world's fastest bird. In a headfirst dive, it can reach speeds of up to 350 km per hour.

## Look For

A pair of peregrines will sometimes nest on the ledge of a tall building, right in the middle of an urban area.

# Sora
*Porzana carolina*

Soras have small bodies and large, chickenlike feet. Even without webbed feet, these unique creatures swim quite well over short distances.
• Two rising *or-Ah or-Ah* whistles followed by a strange, descending whinny indicate that Soras are nearby. Although the Sora is the most common and widespread rail species in North America, it is seldom seen. This secretive bird prefers to remain hidden in dense marshland, but it will occasionally venture into the shallows to search for aquatic insects and molluscs.

**Other ID:** black face, throat and foreneck; grey neck and breast; long wings and tail.
**Size:** *L* 20–25 cm; *W* 35 cm.
**Voice:** alarm call is a sharp *keek*; courtship song begins *or-Ah or-Ah* followed by a maniacal, descending *weee-weee-weee*.
**Status:** uncommon to common migrant and breeder.
**Habitat:** wetlands with abundant emergent cattails, bulrushes, sedges and grasses.

## Similar Birds

Virginia Rail

Yellow Rail

brown-and-white-speckled back and upperwings

short, yellow bill

long, greenish legs

*breeding*

**Nesting:** usually over water or in a wet meadow; well-built basket nest of grass and aquatic vegetation; darkly speckled, buff or olive buff eggs are 31 x 22 mm; pair incubates 10–12 eggs for 18–20 days.

### Did You Know?

Literally as "thin as a rail," the Sora has a very narrow body that allows it to squeeze through thick stands of cattails.

### Look For

The Sora has long legs, a stumpy body and almost no neck. It bustles through the shallows, darting in and out of the reeds.

# American Coot
*Fulica americana*

You might mistake this bird for a duck, and with good reason. It dabbles on the water and feeds confidently on land, but is actually part of the rail family. • During its breeding season, this bird's behaviour confirms the expression, "crazy as a coot." It is aggressively territorial and constantly squabbles with other waterbirds in its space. • Though their webbed feet allow them to dive, these birds are not afraid to steal a meal from another skilled diver who brings a succulent piece of water celery to the surface.

**Other ID:** ducklike bird; long, green yellow legs; lobed toes.
**Size:** *L* 33–41 cm; *W* 60 cm.
**Voice:** calls frequently in summer, day and night: *kuk-kuk-kuk-kuk-kuk;* also grunts.
**Status:** common to very common migrant and breeder; some overwinter on open water.
**Habitat:** *Breeding:* shallow marshes, ponds and wetlands with open water and emergent vegetation. *In migration* and *winter:* urban ponds and golf courses.

## Similar Birds

Black Scoter

Pied-billed Grebe

red eyes

reddish spot
on white
forehead shield

grey black body

white,
chickenlike bill
with dark ring
around tip

*adult*

**Nesting:** in emergent vegetation; pair builds
floating nest of cattails and grass; buffy white,
brown-spotted eggs are 49 x 34 mm; pair incubates 8–12 eggs for 21–25 days; broods twice.

## Did You Know?

American Coots are also
known as "Mud Hens."

## Look For

You might catch a glimpse
of these birds' antics during
breeding season as they
scoot across the water,
flailing their wings and
splashing their opponents.

# Sandhill Crane
*Grus canadensis*

The Sandhill Crane's deep, rattling call can be heard long before this bird passes overhead. Its coiled trachea alters the pitch of its voice, making it sound louder and carry farther. • At first glance, large, V-shaped flocks of Sandhill Cranes can look like flocks of Canada Geese, but the cranes often soar and circle in the air, and they do not honk like geese. • Cranes mate for life and reinforce pair bonds each spring with an elaborate courtship dance. The ritual looks much like human dancing, which may seem like a strange comparison until you witness the spectacle firsthand.

**Other ID:** white "cheek" and "chin"; dark legs; plumage is often stained rusty red from iron oxides in water.
**Size:** *L* 1–1.3 m; *W* 1.8–2.1 m.
**Voice:** loud, resonant, rattling: *gu-rrroo gu-rrroo gurrroo.*
**Status:** uncommon migrant and breeder.
**Habitat:** open ground, fields, lakeshores, sandy beaches, mudflats, gravel streambeds, wet meadows and grasslands.

## Similar Birds

Whooping Crane

Great Blue Heron (p. 44)

naked, red crown

long, straight bill

long neck

grey overall

*adult*

**Nesting:** in the water or along the shoreline on a large mound of aquatic vegetation; brown-blotched, buff eggs are 94 x 60 mm; pair incubates 2 eggs for 29–32 days; egg hatching is staggered.

## Did You Know?

Flocks of migrating Sandhill Cranes are usually made up of close family members.

## Look For

Although most cranes are seen during migration, many of them nest in Alberta's foothills and boreal forest, in secluded fens, bogs and marshes.

# Killdeer
*Charadrius vociferus*

The boisterous Killdeer always attracts attention. It is a gifted actor, well known for its "broken wing" distraction display. When an intruder wanders too close to its nest, it is greeted by an adult, who cries piteously while dragging a wing and stumbling about as if injured. Most predators take the bait and follow, and once the Killdeer has lured the predator far away from its nest, it miraculously recovers from the injury and flies off with a loud call.

**Other ID:** white face patch above bill; black forehead band; tail projects beyond wing tips. *Immature:* downy; only 1 breast band.
**Size:** L 23–28 cm; W 61 cm.
**Voice:** loud and distinctive *kill-dee kill-dee kill-deer;* variations include *deer-deer.*
**Status:** common to very common migrant and breeder.
**Habitat:** open ground, fields, lakeshores, sandy beaches, mudflats, gravel streambeds, wet meadows and grasslands.

## Similar Birds

Semipalmated Plover

Piping Plover

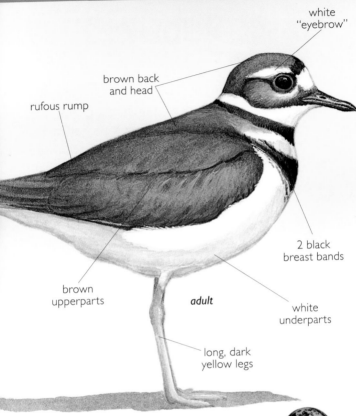

white "eyebrow"

brown back and head

rufous rump

2 black breast bands

brown upperparts

*adult*

white underparts

long, dark yellow legs

**Nesting:** on open ground, in a shallow, usually unlined depression; heavily speckled, creamy buff eggs are 36 x 27 mm; pair incubates 4 eggs for 24–28 days; may raise 2 broods.

## Did You Know?

In spring, you might hear a European Starling imitate the vocal Killdeer's call.

## Look For

The Killdeer has adapted well to urbanization, and inhabits golf courses and abandoned industrial areas as often as shorelines.

# Lesser Yellowlegs
*Tringa flavipes*

The "tattletale" Lesser Yellowlegs is the self-appointed sentinel in a mixed flock of shorebirds, raising the alarm at the first sign of a threat. • It is challenging to discern Lesser Yellowlegs and Greater Yellowlegs in the field, but with practice, you will notice that the Lesser's bill is finer, straighter and about as long as its head is wide. With long legs and wings, the Lesser appears slimmer and taller than the Greater, and it is more commonly seen in flocks. Finally, the Lesser Yellowlegs emits a pair of peeps, while the Greater peeps three times.

**Other ID:** dark eye line; fine, dense, dark streaking on head, neck and breast; light lores.
**Size:** *L* 25–28 mm; *W* 61 cm.
**Voice:** typically a high-pitched pair of *tew* notes; noisiest on breeding grounds.
**Status:** common to very common migrant and breeder.
**Habitat:** *Breeding:* grassy ponds and open forest. *In migration:* shorelines of lakes, rivers, marshes and ponds.

## Similar Birds

Willet

Greater Yellowlegs

Solitary Sandpiper

*nonbreeding*

brownish black, mottled back and upperwing

all-dark bill is about the width of head

lacks barring on belly

bright yellow legs

*breeding*

**Nesting:** in open muskeg or a natural forest opening; in a depression on a dry mound lined with leaves and grass; darkly blotched, buff to olive eggs are 42 x 29 mm; pair incubates 4 eggs for 22–23 days.

## Did You Know?

Yellowlegs were a popular gamebird in the late 1800s because they were plentiful and easy to shoot.

## Look For

The Lesser Yellowlegs wades into the water almost to its belly, sweeping its bill back and forth just below the water's surface.

# Spotted Sandpiper

*Actitis macularius*

The female Spotted Sandpiper, unlike most other female birds, lays her eggs and leaves the male to tend the clutch. Free of responsibility, she flies off to mate again. Only about one percent of birds display this unusual breeding strategy known as polyandry. Each summer, the female can lay up to four clutches and is capable of producing 20 eggs. As the season progresses, however, available males become harder to find. Come August, there may be seven females for every available male.

**Other ID:** dark eye line. *Nonbreeding* and *immature:* pure white breast, foreneck and throat; brown bill; dull yellow legs.
**Size:** *L* 18–20 cm; W 38 cm.
**Voice:** sharp, crisp *eat-wheat, eat-wheat, wheat-wheat-wheat-wheat.*
**Status:** common migrant and breeder.
**Habitat:** shorelines, gravel beaches, ponds, marshes, alluvial wetlands, rivers, streams, swamps and sewage lagoons; occasionally seen in cultivated fields.

## Similar Birds

Solitary Sandpiper

### Did You Know?

Sandpipers have four toes: three point forward and one points backward. Plovers, such as Killdeer, have only three toes.

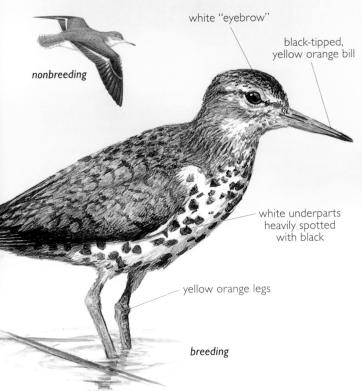

white "eyebrow"

black-tipped, yellow orange bill

*nonbreeding*

white underparts heavily spotted with black

yellow orange legs

*breeding*

**Nesting:** usually near water; sheltered by vegetation; shallow scrape is lined with grass; darkly blotched, creamy buff eggs are 33 x 24 mm; male incubates 4 eggs for 20–24 days and raises the young.

## Look For

Spotted Sandpipers have a few identifying characteristics such as their habit of continuously bobbing their tails and teetering. Also, look for their white upperwing stripe and rapid, shallow wingbeats as they fly close to the water's surface.

# Wilson's Snipe
*Gallinago delicata*

A courting Wilson's Snipe makes an eerie, winnowing sound, like a rapidly hooting owl. The male's specialized outer tail feathers vibrate rapidly in the air as he performs daring, headfirst dives high above a wetland. During the spring, snipes can be heard displaying day and night. • When flushed from cover, these birds perform a series of aerial zigzags to confuse predators. Because of this habit, hunters who were skilled enough to shoot snipes became known as "snipers," a term later adopted by the military.

**Other ID:** heavily striped head, back, neck and breast. *In flight:* quick zigzags on takeoff.
**Size:** L 27–29 cm; W 46 cm.
**Voice:** in flight, courtship song is an eerie, accelerating *woo-woo-woo-woo-woo-woo;* often sings *wheat wheat wheat* from an elevated perch; alarm call is a nasal *scaip.*
**Status:** common migrant and breeder; a few may overwinter near open water.
**Habitat:** cattail and bulrush marshes, sedge meadows, poorly drained floodplains, bogs and fens; willow and red-osier dogwood tangles.

## Similar Birds

Short-billed Dowitcher

Long-billed Dowitcher

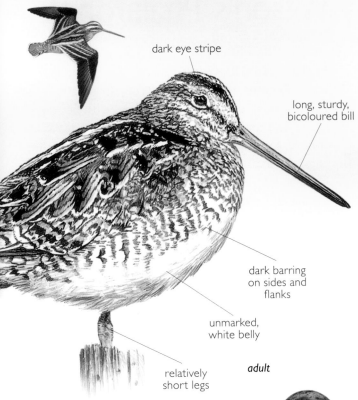

dark eye stripe

long, sturdy, bicoloured bill

dark barring on sides and flanks

unmarked, white belly

relatively short legs

*adult*

**Nesting:** usually in dry grass; nest is made of grass, moss and leaves; darkly marked, olive buff to brown eggs are 39 x 28 mm; female incubates 4 eggs for 18–20 days.

### Did You Know?

Both parents raise the snipe nestlings, often splitting the brood, with each parent caring for half the chicks.

### Look For

A snipe often plunges its entire head underwater while probing the shallows for tasty aquatic critters.

# Wilson's Phalarope
*Phalaropus tricolor*

Phalaropes are like wind-up toys: they spin and whirl about in tight circles, stirring up aquatic insects and small crustaceans. Then, with needle-like bills, they pluck their prey from the water as it funnels toward the surface. • While incubating the eggs, the male phalarope sheds the feathers on his belly and develops a thick skin on his underside. This "brood patch" swells with blood and provides the right temperature for incubation. In most other species, the female develops the brood patch.

**Other ID:** black legs. *Breeding female:* very sharp colours; white "eyebrow," throat and nape. *Breeding male:* duller plumage overall; dark "cap." *Nonbreeding:* all-grey upperparts; white "eyebrow" and grey eye line; white underparts; dark yellowish or greenish legs.
**Size:** *L* 22–24 cm; *W* 43 cm.
**Voice:** deep, grunting *work work* or *wu wu wu*, usually given on the breeding grounds.
**Status:** uncommon to common migrant and breeder.
**Habitat:** *Breeding:* cattail marshes and grass or sedge margins of sewage lagoons. *In migration:* lakeshores, marshes and sewage lagoons.

## Similar Birds

Red-necked Phalarope

Red Phalarope

black eye line extends down side of neck

dark, needlelike bill

grey "cap"

♂

chestnut brown sides of neck

♀

*breeding*

light underparts

**Nesting:** often near water; well concealed in a depression lined with vegetation; brown-blotched, buff eggs are 37 x 24 mm; male incubates 4 eggs for 18–27 days and rears the young.

## Did You Know?

Phalaropes are polyandrous: the female mates with several males. After laying eggs, she abandons her mate and the eggs.

## Look For

Unlike most birds, the female phalarope is more colourful than the male. The male phalarope's dull colours help camouflage him while he incubates the eggs.

# Franklin's Gull
*Larus pipixcan*

The Franklin's Gull is not a typical "sea gull." This land-loving bird spends much of its life inland and it nests on the prairies, where it is affectionately known as the "Prairie Dove." It often follows tractors across agricultural fields, snatching up insects from the tractor's path in much the same way as its cousins follow fishing boats. • The Franklin's Gull is one of only two gull species that migrate long distances between breeding and wintering grounds—the majority of Franklin's Gulls winter along the Pacific coast of Peru and Chile.

**Other ID:** grey mantle; black wing tips with white spots. *Breeding:* breast often has a pinkish tinge. *Nonbreeding:* white head; orange bill; dark patch on the back of the head; white underparts.
**Size:** L 33–38; W 90–95 cm.
**Voice:** mewing, shrill *weeeh-ah weeeh-ah* while feeding and in migration.
**Status:** common migrant and breeder.
**Habitat:** agricultural fields, marshlands, meadows, lakes, rivermouths and landfills.

## Similar Birds

Bonaparte's Gull

Common Tern (p. 78)

*nonbreeding*

black head

white eye ring

red bill

red orange legs

*breeding*

**Nesting:** colonial; usually in dense emergent vegetation; floating platform nest is built above water and lined with fine grass and plant down; pale green to buffy olive, brown-speckled eggs are 52 x 36 mm; pair incubates 3 eggs for 25 days.

## Did You Know?

This gull was named for Sir John Franklin, the British navigator and explorer who led four expeditions to the Arctic in the 19th century.

## Look For

When this bird feels threatened, it tosses its head or extends its head and bill backward. It may also flap extended wings while voicing long, loud calls.

# Ring-billed Gull

*Larus delawarensis*

Few people can claim they have never seen this common and widespread gull. Highly tolerant of humans, Ring-billed Gulls are part of our everyday lives, scavenging our litter and fouling our vehicles. These omnivorous gulls will eat almost anything. They swarm parks, beaches, golf courses and fast-food parking lots looking for food handouts, leading people to consider them pests. However, few species have adjusted to human development as well as the Ring-billed Gull, which is something to appreciate.

**Other ID:** white underparts. *In flight:* black wing tips with a few white spots.
**Size:** *L* 46–51 cm; *W* 1.2 m.
**Voice:** high-pitched *kakakaka-akakaka;* also a low, laughing *yook-yook-yook.*
**Status:** abundant migrant and breeder.
**Habitat:** lakes, rivers, landfills, golf courses, fields and parks.

## Similar Birds

Herring Gull          Glaucous Gull          Thayer's Gull          Iceland Gull

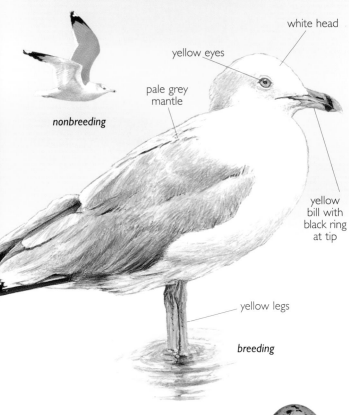

*nonbreeding*

white head

yellow eyes

pale grey mantle

yellow bill with black ring at tip

yellow legs

*breeding*

**Nesting:** colonial; in a shallow scrape on the ground lined with grass, debris and sticks; brown-blotched, grey to olive eggs are 59 x 42 mm; pair incubates 2–4 eggs for 23–28 days.

## Did You Know?

In chaotic nesting colonies, adult Ring-billed Gulls will call out and recognize the response of their chicks.

## Look For

To differentiate between gulls, notice the markings on their bills and the colour of their legs.

# Common Tern
*Sterna hirundo*

Common Terns are sleek, agile birds. They patrol the shorelines of lakes and rivers during spring and fall, settling in large, noisy nesting colonies during the summer months. To win a mate, the male struts through the breeding colony with an offering of fish in his mouth. If a female accepts a suitor's gracious gift, the two make a breeding pair. Parents defend their nest by diving repeatedly and aggressively at intruders, and even defecate on offenders to drive them away!

**Other ID:** white rump. *Breeding:* white tail with grey outer edges. *Nonbreeding:* black nape; lacks black "cap." *In flight:* white underparts; shallow forked tail; long, pointed wings; dark grey wedge near lighter grey upperwing tips.
**Size:** *L* 33–41 cm; *W* 76 cm.
**Voice:** high-pitched, drawn-out *keee-are;* most commonly heard at colonies but also in foraging flights.
**Status:** common migrant and breeder.
**Habitat:** large lakes, open wetlands, slow-moving rivers, islands and beaches.

## Similar Birds

Forster's Tern          Arctic Tern          Caspian Tern

*nonbreeding*

black "cap"

black tip on red bill

red legs

*breeding*

**Nesting:** colonial; on an island; in a small scrape lined with pebbles, vegetation or shells; darkly blotched, creamy white eggs are 42 x 30 mm; pair incubates 1–3 eggs for 20–24 days.

## Did You Know?

Terns are effortless flyers and impressive long-distance migrants. A Common Tern banded in Great Britain was once recovered in Australia.

## Look For

Terns hover over the water, then dive in headfirst to capture small fish or aquatic invertebrates below the surface.

# Black Tern
*Chlidonias niger*

Black Terns rule the skies above cattail marshes. These acrobatic birds wheel about in feeding flights, picking minnows from the water's surface and catching insects in midair.
• Wetland habitat loss and degradation have caused Black Tern populations to decline. As well, these birds are sensitive nesters and will not return to a nesting area if the water level or plant density changes. Wetland conservation efforts may eventually help these birds recover to their former prosperity.

**Other ID:** grey back, tail and wings. *Nonbreeding:* white underparts and forehead; molting fall birds may be mottled with brown. *In flight:* long, pointed wings; shallowly forked tail; reddish black legs; black underparts.
**Size:** L 23–25 cm; W 61 cm.
**Voice:** greeting call is a shrill, metallic *kik-kik-kik-kik-kik;* typical alarm call is *kreea.*
**Status:** common migrant and breeder.
**Habitat:** shallow, freshwater cattail marshes, wetlands, lake edges and sewage ponds with emergent vegetation.

## Similar Birds

Forster's Tern

Common Tern (p. 78)

Caspian Tern

*nonbreeding*

black head

black bill

white undertail coverts

*breeding*

**Nesting:** loosely colonial; flimsy nest of dead plant material is built on floating vegetation, a muddy mound or a muskrat house; darkly blotched olive to pale buff eggs are 34 x 25 mm; pair incubates 3 eggs for 21–22 days.

## Did You Know?

The Black Tern's genus name is a variation of *chelidonias*, the Greek word for "swallow." The name reflects the tern's darting, swallowlike flight pattern.

## Look For

Flocks of Black Terns can be seen snatching insects from the air at dawn and dusk.

# Rock Pigeon
*Columba livia*

The colourful and familiar Rock Pigeons have an unusual feature: they feed their young a substance similar to milk. These birds lack mammary glands, but they secrete "pigeon milk," a nutritious liquid produced in their crops. A chick inserts its bills down the adult's throat to reach the thick, protein-rich fluid. • Rock Pigeons are likely the descendants of a Eurasian bird that was first domesticated around 4500 BC. Rock Pigeons have been used as message couriers by the likes of Caesar and Napoleon, and and as scientific subjects and even as pets.

**Other ID:** orange feet. *In flight:* holds wings in deep "V" while gliding.
**Size:** *L* 31–33 cm; *W* 71 cm.
**Voice:** soft, cooing *coorrr-coorrr-coorrr.*
**Status:** abundant year-round resident.
**Habitat:** urban areas, railway yards and agricultural areas; high cliffs often provide more natural habitat.

## Similar Birds

Mourning Dove (p. 84)

## Look For

No other "wild" bird varies as much in coloration, a result of semi-domestication and extensive inbreeding over time.

colour is highly variable
(iridescent blue grey,
red, white or tan)

dark-tipped tail

usually has
white rump

*adult*

**Nesting:** in a barn or on a cliff, bridge or tower;
in a flimsy nest of sticks, grass and other vegetation;
glossy white eggs are 39 x 29 mm; pair incubates
2 eggs for 16–19 days; may raise broods year-round.

## Did You Know?

Much of our understanding of bird migration, endocrinology,
colour genetics and sensory perception comes from experiments involving Rock Pigeons.

# Mourning Dove

*Zenaida macroura*

The Mourning Dove's soft cooing, which filters through broken woodlands and suburban parks, is often confused with the sound of a hooting owl. Curious birders who track down the source of the calls are often surprised to find the streamlined silhouette of a perched dove. • These popular game animals are one of the most abundant native birds in North America. Their numbers and range have increased since human development created more open habitats and food sources such as waste grain and bird feeders.

**Other ID:** small head; sleek body; dark bill; long, white-trimmed, tapering tail.
**Size:** *L* 28–33 cm; W 46 cm.
**Voice:** mournful, soft, slow *oh-woe-woe-woe*.
**Status:** uncommon to common migrant and breeder.
**Habitat:** open and riparian woodlands, forest edges, agricultural and suburban areas, open parks.

## Similar Birds

Rock Pigeon (p. 82)       Yellow-billed Cuckoo       Black-billed Cuckoo

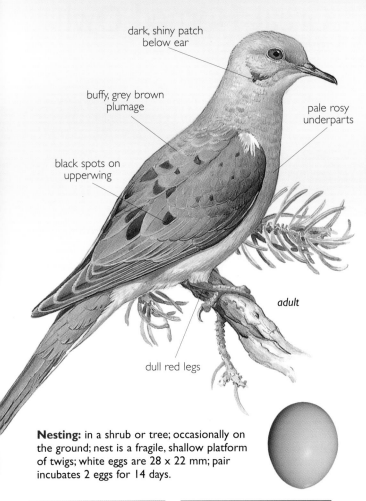

dark, shiny patch below ear

buffy, grey brown plumage

pale rosy underparts

black spots on upperwing

dull red legs

*adult*

**Nesting:** in a shrub or tree; occasionally on the ground; nest is a fragile, shallow platform of twigs; white eggs are 28 x 22 mm; pair incubates 2 eggs for 14 days.

## Did You Know?

The Mourning Dove raises up to six broods each year—more than any other native bird.

## Look For

When the Mourning Dove bursts into flight, its wings clap above and below its body. This bird also creates a whistling sound when flying at a high speed.

# Great Horned Owl
*Bubo virginianus*

This highly adaptable and superbly camouflaged hunter is our provincial bird. The Great Horned Owl has sharp hearing and powerful vision that allow it to hunt at night as well as by day. It will swoop down from a perch onto almost any small creature that moves. • An owl has specially designed feathers on its wings: the leading edge of the first primary feather is serrated rather than smooth. This feature interrupts airflow over the wing and allows the owl to fly noiselessly. • Great Horned Owls have been known to kill and eat Barred Owls, and to displace Bald Eagles from their nests.

**Other ID:** white "chin"; heavily mottled grey, brown and black upperparts; overall plumage varies from light grey to dark brown.
**Size:** L 46–64 cm; W 91–152 cm.
**Voice:** breeding call is 4–6 deep hoots: *hoo-hoo-hoooo hoo-hoo* or *Who's awake? Me too;* male gives higher-pitched hoots.
**Status:** common year-round resident.
**Habitat:** fragmented forests, fields, riparian woodlands, suburban parks and wooded edges of landfills.

## Similar Birds

Long-eared Owl

Great Gray Owl

Short-eared Owl

yellow eyes

tall, widely spaced "ear" tufts form a triangle with beak

rusty orange facial disc is outlined in black

fine, horizontal barring on breast

*adult*

**Nesting:** in another bird's abandoned stick nest or in a tree cavity; adds little or no nest material; dull whitish eggs are 56 x 47 mm; mostly the female incubates 2–3 eggs for 28–35 days.

## Did You Know?

The Great Horned Owl has a poor sense of smell, which might explain why it is the only consistent predator of skunks.

## Look For

Owls regurgitate pellets that contain the indigestible parts of their prey. You can find these pellets under frequently used perches.

# Snowy Owl
*Bubo scandiacus*

Feathered to the toes, the ghostly white Snowy Owl can remain active even in frigid winter temperatures. Its transparent plumage traps heat like a greenhouse. This bird also creates insulating air pockets between its body and the cold air by ruffling its feathers.
• Snowy Owls are regular annual visitors in Alberta, but their numbers can fluctuate dramatically. When lemming and vole populations crash in the Arctic, large numbers of Snowy Owls venture south to search for food. • As Snowy Owls age, their plumage pales—older males are often pure white.

**Other ID:** *Male:* almost entirely white with very little dark flecking. *Immature:* heavier barring than adult female.
**Size:** *L* 51–69 cm; *W* 1.4–1.7 m (female is noticeably larger).
**Voice:** quiet during winter.
**Status:** uncommon to common in migration and winter.
**Habitat:** open country, including croplands, meadows and lakeshores; often perches on fence posts, buildings and utility poles.

## Similar Birds

Northern Hawk Owl

Great Gray Owl

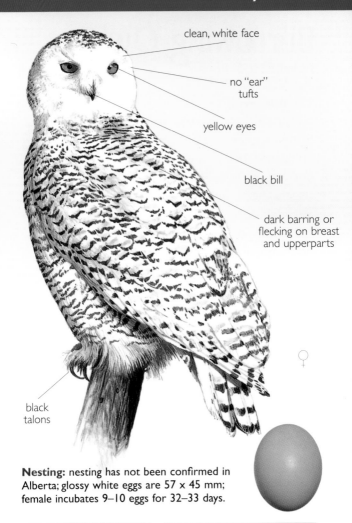

clean, white face

no "ear" tufts

yellow eyes

black bill

dark barring or flecking on breast and upperparts

black talons

**Nesting:** nesting has not been confirmed in Alberta; glossy white eggs are 57 x 45 mm; female incubates 9–10 eggs for 32–33 days.

### Did You Know?

The Snowy Owl may have inspired the first bird painting. Depictions of this bird have been found in prehistoric cave art.

### Look For

An owl often swoops down from its perch and punches through the snow to capture a rodent, leaving an imprint of its outstretched wings.

# Burrowing Owl
*Athene cunicularia*

The Burrowing Owl is a loyal prairie inhabitant. Its favourite haunts are heavily grazed pastures in cultivated regions and disturbed areas in extensive grasslands. It nests in abandoned underground burrows, and the extermination of ground squirrels on the prairies has greatly reduced the number of suitable owl nesting sites. Agricultural chemicals, collisions with vehicles and the conversion of native grasslands to cropland are thought to be some of the other challenges facing this endangered bird.

**Other ID:** bold, white "chin" stripe; brown upperparts are flecked with white.
**Size:** *L* 23–28 cm; *W* 50–60 cm.
**Voice:** call is a harsh *chuk;* chattering *quick-quick-quick;* rattlesnake-like warning call when inside its burrow. *Male: coo-hooo* courtship call is higher than, but similar to, the Mourning Dove's *coo.*
**Status:** rare migrant and breeder.
**Habitat:** open, short-grass haylands, pastures and prairies; occasionally on lawns and golf courses.

## Similar Birds

Short-eared Owl

Northern Saw-whet Owl
(p. 92)

rounded head

yellow bill

no "ear" tufts

white around eyes

horizontal barring on underparts

long legs

short tail

*adult*

**Nesting:** singly or in loose colonies; in an abandoned natural or artificial burrow; nest is lined with bits of dry manure, food debris, feathers and fine grass; white eggs are 21 x 26 mm; female incubates 5–11 eggs for 27–30 days.

## Did You Know?

The Burrowing Owl's range and population numbers have decreased drastically in recent years.

## Look For

During the day, these owls perch on fence posts or at the entrance to their burrows, where they look very similar to ground squirrels.

# Northern Saw-whet Owl
*Aegolius acadicus*

The tiny Northern Saw-whet Owl makes the most of every hunting opportunity. When temperatures fall below freezing and prey is abundant, the Saw-whet will catch more than it can eat. It usually stores the extra food in trees and allows it to freeze. When hunting efforts fail, the hungry owl returns to thaw out the frozen cache, "incubating" the food as if it were a clutch of eggs! The Saw-whet's favourite foods include mice, voles, large insects and songbirds.

**Other ID:** dark bill; pale, unbordered facial disc; white-spotted, brown upperparts. *Juvenile:* white patch between eyes; rich brown head and breast; buff brown belly.
**Size:** *L* 18–23 cm; *W* 43–55 cm.
**Voice:** whistled, evenly spaced *whew-whew*, repeated about 100 times per minute.
**Status:** uncommon to common year-round.
**Habitat:** coniferous and mixed forests; wooded city parks and ravines.

## Similar Birds

Boreal Owl

Eastern Screech-Owl

Northern Hawk Owl

white-streaked forehead

large, rounded head

vertical, rusty streaks on underparts

small body

short tail

*adult*

**Nesting:** in a natural tree hollow or a nest box; white eggs are 30 x 25 mm; female incubates 5–6 eggs for 27–29 days; male feeds the female during incubation.

## Did You Know?

This owl's name refers to its call, which sounds like a saw blade being sharpened or the "bleeping" sound of a truck backing up.

## Look For

One way to detect the Northern Saw-whet Owl is by looking for "whitewash," or buildups of excrement, under roosting sites.

# Common Nighthawk
*Chordeiles minor*

The Common Nighthawk makes an unforgettable booming sound as it flies high overhead. In an energetic courting display, the male dives, then swerves skyward, making a hollow *vroom* sound with its wings. • Like other members of the night-jar family, the Common Nighthawk has adapted to catch insects in midair: its gaping mouth is surrounded by feather shafts that funnel insects into its beak. A nighthawk can eat over 2600 insects, including mosquitoes, blackflies and flying ants, in one day.

**Other ID:** *Female:* buff throat. *In flight:* bold, white "wrist" patches on long, pointed wings; shallowly forked, barred tail; erratic flight.
**Size:** *L* 22–25 cm; *W* 61 cm.
**Voice:** frequently repeated, nasal *peent peent;* wings make a deep, hollow *boom* during courtship dive.
**Status:** uncommon to common migrant and breeder.
**Habitat:** *Breeding:* forest openings, burns, bogs, rocky outcroppings and gravel rooftops. *In migration:* often near water; any area with large numbers of flying insects.

## Similar Birds

Common Poorwill

## Look For

With their short legs and tiny feet, Nighthawks sit lengthwise on tree branches and blend in with the bark.

♂

white throat
on male

cryptic, mottled
plumage

barred underparts

♂

**Nesting:** on bare ground; no nest is built; heavily marked, creamy white to buff eggs are 30 x 22 mm; female incubates 2 eggs for about 19 days; both adults feed the young.

## Did You Know?

It was once believed that members of the nightjar, or "goat-sucker," family could suck milk from the udders of goats, causing the goats to go blind!

# Ruby-throated Hummingbird

*Archilochus colubris*

Ruby-throated Hummingbirds bridge the ecological gap between birds and bees—they feed on sweet, energy-rich flower nectar and pollinate the flowers in the process. A sugarwater feeder or native, nectar-producing flowers such as honeysuckle can attract hummingbirds to your backyard. In straight-ahead flight, hummingbirds beat their wings up to 80 times per second, and their hearts can beat up to 1200 times per minute!

**Other ID:** *Male:* iridescent green back. *Female* and *immature:* fine, dark throat streaking.
**Size:** *L* 9 cm; *W* 11 cm.
**Voice:** most noticeable is the soft buzzing of the wings while in flight; also produces a loud *chick* and other high squeaks.
**Status:** uncommon spring migrant and breeder.
**Habitat:** open, mixed woodlands, wetlands, orchards, tree-lined meadows, flower gardens and backyards with trees and feeders.

## Similar Birds

Rufous Hummingbird

## Look For

The hummingbird is among the few birds that can fly vertically and in reverse.

needlelike bill

pale underparts

♀

♂

black "chin"
with ruby red
throat on male

iridescent,
green back

dark tail

**Nesting:** on a horizontal tree limb; tiny, deep cup
nest of plant down and fibres is held together
with spider silk; lichens and leaves are pasted on
the exterior walls; white eggs are 13 x 8 mm;
female incubates 2 eggs for 13–16 days.

## Did You Know?

Each year, Ruby-throated Hummingbirds migrate across the
Gulf of Mexico, a nonstop 800-km journey. Weighing about as
much as a nickel, a hummingbird can briefly reach speeds of
up to 100 km per hour!

# Belted Kingfisher
*Ceryle alcyon*

Perched on a bare branch over a productive pool, the Belted Kingfisher utters a scratchy, rattling call. Then, with little regard for its scruffy hairdo, the "king of the fishes" plunges headfirst into the water and snags a fish or a frog. Back on land, the kingfisher flips its prey into the air and swallows it headfirst.
• Kingfisher pairs nest on sandy banks, taking turns digging a tunnel with their sturdy bills and claws. Nest burrows may measure up to two metres long and are often found near water.

**Other ID:** small white patch near eye; white "collar"; bluish upperparts; white underwings; short legs.
**Size:** *L* 28–36 cm; *W* 51 cm.
**Voice:** fast, repetitive, cackling rattle, like a teacup shaking on a saucer.
**Status:** uncommon to common migrant and breeder; a few overwinter.
**Habitat:** rivers, large streams, lakes, marshes and beaver ponds, especially near exposed soil banks, gravel pits or bluffs.

## Similar Birds

Blue Jay (p. 116)

### Look For

With an extra red band across her belly, the female kingfisher is more colourful than her mate.

shaggy crest

long, straight bill

♀

♂

blue grey breast band

rust-coloured "belt" on female (may be incomplete)

no "belt"

**Nesting:** in a cavity at the end of an earth burrow; glossy white eggs are 34 x 27 mm; pair incubates 6–7 eggs for 22–24 days; both adults feed the young.

## Did You Know?

In Greek mythology, Alcyon, the daughter of the wind god, grieved so deeply for her drowned husband that the gods transformed them both into kingfishers.

# Downy Woodpecker

*Picoides pubescens*

A pair of Downy Woodpeckers at your backyard bird feeder will brighten a frosty winter day. These approachable little birds are more tolerant of human activities than most other species, and they visit feeders more often than the larger, more aggressive Hairy Woodpeckers *(P. villosus)*. • Like other woodpeckers, the Downy has evolved special features to help cushion the shock of repeated hammering, including a strong bill and neck muscles, a flexible, reinforced skull and a brain that is tightly packed in its protective cranium.

**Other ID:** black eye line and crown; white belly; mostly black tail. *Female:* mostly black tail.
**Size:** *L* 15–18 cm; *W* 30 cm.
**Voice:** long, unbroken trill; calls are a sharp *pik* or *ki-ki-ki* or whiny *queek queek*.
**Status:** common year-round.
**Habitat:** any wooded environment, especially deciduous and mixed forests and areas with tall, deciduous shrubs.

## Similar Birds

Hairy Woodpecker

American Three-toed Woodpecker

Yellow-bellied Sapsucker

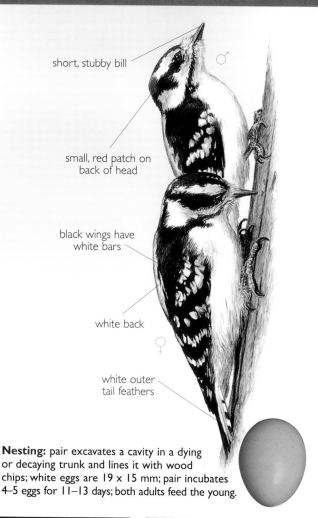

short, stubby bill

♂

small, red patch on
back of head

black wings have
white bars

white back

♀

white outer
tail feathers

**Nesting:** pair excavates a cavity in a dying
or decaying trunk and lines it with wood
chips; white eggs are 19 x 15 mm; pair incubates
4–5 eggs for 11–13 days; both adults feed the young.

## Did You Know?

Woodpeckers have feath-
ered nostrils, which filter
out the sawdust produced
when hammering trees.

## Look For

The Downy Woodpecker
uses its small bill to probe
tiny crevices for invertebrates
and wood-boring grubs.

# Northern Flicker
*Colaptes auratus*

Instead of boring holes in trees, the Northern Flicker scours the ground in search of invertebrates, particularly ants. With robinlike hops, it investigates anthills, grassy meadows and forest clearings. • Flickers often bathe in dusty depressions. The dust particles absorb oils and bacteria that can harm the birds' feathers. To clean themselves even more thoroughly, flickers squash captured ants and preen themselves with the remains. Ants contain formic acid, which kills small parasites on the flickers' skin and feathers.

**Other ID:** spotted, buff to whitish underparts; white rump; long bill; brownish to buff face; grey crown.
**Size:** *L* 32–33 cm; *W* 51 cm.
**Voice:** loud, laughing, rapid *kick-kick-kick-kick-kick-kick; woika-woika-woika* issued during courtship.
**Status:** common migrant and breeder.
**Habitat:** open deciduous, mixed and coniferous woodlands and forest edges, fields, meadows, beaver ponds and other wetlands.

## Similar Birds

Yellow-bellied
Sapsucker

## Look For

Woodpeckers use their stiff tail feathers to prop up their bodies while they scale trees and excavate cavities.

barred, brown
back and wings

black "moustache"
stripe

♂

black "bib"

red nape
crescent

no "moustache"

♀

yellow underwings
and undertail

**Nesting:** pair excavates a cavity in a dying or
decaying trunk and lines it with wood chips; may
also use a nest box; white eggs are 28 x 22 mm;
pair incubates 5–8 eggs for 11–16 days.

## Did You Know?

Many woodpeckers have zygodactyl feet—two toes face
forward and two point backward. This structure allows them
to move vertically up and down tree trunks.

# Pileated Woodpecker
*Dryocopus pileatus*

The Pileated Woodpecker, with its flaming red crest, chisel-like bill and commanding size, requires 40 hectares of mature forest as a home territory. Pairs settle in mature forests and spend up to six weeks excavating a large nest cavity in a dead or decaying tree. • A woodpecker's bill becomes shorter as the bird ages. In his historic painting of the Pileated Woodpecker, John J. Audubon correctly depicted the juvenile birds with slightly longer bills than the adults.

**Other ID:** predominantly black; white wing linings; white "chin." *Female:* no red "moustache"; grey brown forehead.
**Size:** L 41–48 cm; W 74 cm.
**Voice:** loud, fast, rolling *woika-woika-woika-woika;* long series of *kuk* notes; loud, resonant drumming.
**Status:** uncommon to common year-round.
**Habitat:** mature, deciduous, mixed or coniferous forests; also riparian woodlands or woodlots in suburban and agricultural areas.

## Similar Birds

Yellow-bellied
Sapsucker

Red-headed
Woodpecker

♂

red crest
(extends from bill
to nape)

stout,
dark bill

red "moustache"

yellow eyes

white stripe
(extends from
bill to shoulder)

♀

*adult pair*

**Nesting:** pair excavates a cavity in a dying or
decaying trunk and lines it with wood chips;
white eggs are 33 x 25 mm; pair incubates 4 eggs
for 15–18 days; both adults feed the young.

## Did You Know?

Ducks, small falcons,
owls and even flying
squirrels frequently nest
in abandoned Pileated
Woodpecker cavities.

## Look For

Foraging Pileated Wood-
peckers leave rectangular
cavities and large holes at
the base of trees.

# Least Flycatcher

*Empidonax minimus*

This bird might not look like a bully, but the Least Flycatcher is one of the boldest and most pugnacious songbirds of our deciduous woodlands. • It is among the most common and widespread *Empidonax* flycatchers in the province. • During the nesting season, it is noisy and conspicuous, forcefully repeating its simple, two-part *che-bek* call throughout much of the day. Intense song battles normally eliminate the need for physical aggression, but feathers fly in occasional disputes over territory and courtship privileges.

**Other ID:** mostly dark bill has yellow orange lower base; grey white to yellowish belly and undertail coverts.
**Size:** L 12–14 cm; W 20 cm.
**Voice:** *Male:* song is a constantly repeated, dry *che-bek che-bek*.
**Status:** common spring migrant and breeder.
**Habitat:** open deciduous or mixed woodlands; forest openings and edges; often in 2nd-growth woodlands and occasionally near human habitation.

## Similar Birds

Alder Flycatcher

Willow Flycatcher

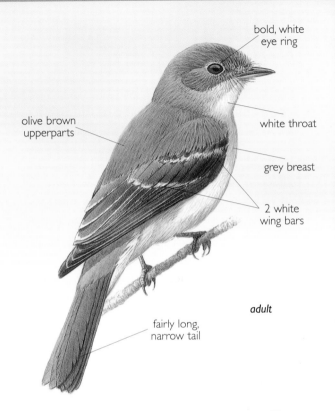

bold, white eye ring

olive brown upperparts

white throat

grey breast

2 white wing bars

*adult*

fairly long, narrow tail

**Nesting:** in the crotch or fork of a small tree or shrub, often against the trunk; female builds a small cup nest of plant fibres and bark lined with fine grass, plant down and feathers; creamy white eggs are 16 x13 mm; female incubates 4 eggs for 13–15 days; both adults feed the young.

## Did You Know?

*Empidonax* flycatchers are aptly named: the literal translation is "mosquito king" and refers to their insect-hunting prowess.

## Look For

A feeding flycatcher will sit on a branch, launch out suddenly to snap up an insect, and then loop back to land on the same perch.

# Eastern Kingbird
## *Tyrannus tyrannus*

The Eastern Kingbird fearlessly attacks crows, hawks and even humans that pass through its territory, pursuing and pecking at them until it feels the threat has passed. No one familiar with the Eastern Kingbird's quarrelsome behaviour will refute its scientific name, *Tyrannus tyrannus*. • Eastern Kingbirds are common and widespread. On a drive in the country you will likely spot at least one of these birds sitting on a fence or utility wire. • This bird eats over 200 kinds of insects and will hover above shrubs or trees to pick berries.

**Other ID:** no eye ring; black legs.
**Size:** *L* 22 cm; *W* 38 cm.
**Voice:** call is a quick, loud, chattering *kit-kit-kitter-kitter;* also a *buzzy dzee-dzee-dzee.*
**Status:** locally common in spring migration and breeding.
**Habitat:** open areas with willow and birch shrubs, agricultural areas and riparian regions, roadsides, burned areas and near human settlement.

## Similar Birds

Olive-sided
Flycatcher

Western Kingbird

small head crest

thin orange red crown
(rarely seen)

dark grey to black
upperparts

black bill

white
underparts

*adult*

white-tipped tail

**Nesting:** on a horizontal limb, stump or upturned tree root; cup nest is made of weeds, twigs and grass; darkly blotched, white to pinkish white eggs are 24 x 18 mm; female incubates 3–4 eggs for 14–18 days.

## Did You Know?

Eastern Kingbirds rarely walk or hop on the ground—they prefer to fly, even for very short distances.

## Look For

The Eastern Kingbird reveals its gentler side in a quivering, butterflylike courtship flight.

# Northern Shrike
*Lanius excubitor*

One of the most vicious predators in the songbird world, the Northern Shrike relies on its sharp, hooked bill to catch and kill small birds or rodents. Its tendency to impale its prey on thorns and barbs for later consumption has earned it the name "Butcher Bird." A shrike may gulp down prey whole and later disgorge undigestable matted feathers and bones in the form of a pellet. Northern Shrikes have also been documented to kill other birds without any intention of eating them.

**Other ID:** pale grey upperparts. *In flight:* white-edged tail; white wing patches.
**Size:** L 25 cm; W 37 cm.
**Voice:** usually silent; occasionally gives a long, grating laugh: *raa-raa-raa-raa*.
**Status:** uncommon to erratic migrant and winter visitor; rare breeder.
**Habitat:** open country, including fields, shrubby areas, forest clearings and roadsides.

## Similar Birds

Loggerhead Shrike

Northern Mockingbird

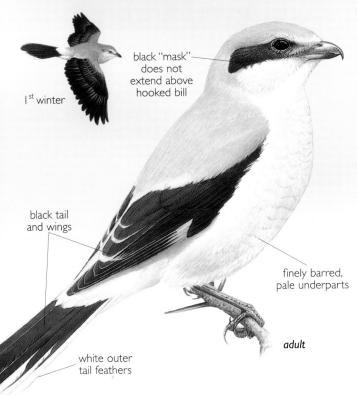

1st winter

black "mask" does not extend above hooked bill

black tail and wings

finely barred, pale underparts

adult

white outer tail feathers

**Nesting:** on the taiga in a spruce, willow or shrub; bulky nest is made of sticks, bark and moss; greenish white to buff-coloured eggs with reddish brown spotting are 29 x 19 mm; female incubates 4–7 eggs for 15–17 days.

## Did You Know?

Shrikes are the world's only true carnivorous songbirds. Africa and Eurasia boast the greatest diversity of shrike species.

## Look For

Northern Shrikes typically perch at the tops of tall trees to survey the surrounding area for prey.

# Red-eyed Vireo
*Vireo olivaceus*

The male Red-eyed Vireo can out-sing any one of his courting neighbours. Capable of delivering about 40 phrases per minute, one tenacious male set a record by singing 21,000 in one day! Though you may still hear the Red-eyed Vireo singing five or six hours after other songbirds have ceased for the day, this bird conceals itself well in its olive brown plumage amongst the foliage of deciduous trees. Its unique red eyes, unusual among songbirds, are even trickier to spot without a good pair of binoculars.

**Other ID:** dark eye line; black-bordered, olive "cheek"; olive green upperparts.
**Size:** *L* 15 cm; *W* 24 cm.
**Voice:** call is a short, scolding *neeah. Male:* song is a series of quick, continuous, variable phrases with pauses in between: *look-up, way-up, tree-top, see-me, here-I-am!*
**Status:** common migrant and breeder.
**Habitat:** deciduous woodlands with a shrubby understorey.

## Similar Birds

Philadelphia Vireo

Tennessee Warbler

Warbling Vireo

black-bordered, blue grey crown

white "eyebrow"

red eyes

white to pale grey underparts

*breeding*

**Nesting:** in a tree or shrub; hanging cup nest is made of grass, roots, spider silk and cocoons; darkly spotted, white eggs are 20 x 14 mm; female incubates 4 eggs for 11–14 days.

## Did You Know?

When parasitized by Brown-headed Cowbirds, Red-eyed Vireos either abandon their nests or raise the cowbird young with their own.

## Look For

The Red-eyed Vireo perches with a hunched stance and hops with its body turned diagonally to its direction of travel.

# Gray Jay
*Perisoreus canadensis*

The friendly, mischievous Gray Jay sports a dark grey cloak and a long, elegant tail. These bold birds form strong pair bonds, and after an absence, partners will seek each other out and touch or nibble bills.
• Gray Jays lay their eggs and begin incubation as early as late February, allowing the young to get a head start on learning to forage and store food. These birds cache food for the winter, and their specialized salivary glands coat the food with a sticky mucus that helps to preserve it.

**Other ID:** fluffy, pale grey plumage; white undertail coverts; white forehead and throat.
**Size:** *L* 28–33 cm; *W* 45 cm.
**Voice:** calls include a soft, whistled *quee-oo,* a chuckled *cla-cla-cla* and a *churr*; also imitates other birds.
**Status:** common year-round.
**Habitat:** dense and open coniferous and mixed forests, bogs and fens; picnic sites and campgrounds.

## Similar Birds

Northern Shrike (p. 110)

Northern Mockingbird

Loggerhead Shrike

white "cheek"

dark bill

dark grey nape and upperparts

light grey breast and belly

adult

long tail

**Nesting:** in a conifer; insulated nest of plant fibres, roots, moss, twigs, feathers and fur; speckled, pale grey to greenish eggs are 29 x 21 mm; female incubates 3–4 eggs for 17–22 days.

## Did You Know?

The Gray Jay's nickname "Whiskey Jack" comes from its Algonquin name, *wis-kat-jon;* other names include "Canada Jay" and "Camp Robber."

## Look For

In flight, the Gray Jay has a distinctive bounce with alternating fast flaps and short glides, usually close to the ground.

# Blue Jay
## *Cyanocitta cristata*

The Blue Jay is easily recognizable with its white-flecked wing feathers and sharply defined facial features. Only the Black-billed Magpie is more vocal. This major league mascot can be quite aggressive when competing for sunflower seeds and peanuts at backyard feeding stations, and it rarely hesitates to drive away smaller birds, squirrels or even cats when it feels threatened. Even the Great Horned Owl is not too formidable a predator for a group of these brave, boisterous mobsters to harass.

**Other ID:** black "necklace"; white bar and flecking on wings.
**Size:** *L* 28–31 cm; *W* 40 cm.
**Voice:** noisy, screaming *jay-jay-jay*; nasal *queedle queedle queedle-queedle* sounds like a muted trumpet; often imitates various sounds, including calls of other birds.
**Status:** common year-round.
**Habitat:** mixed deciduous forests, agricultural areas, scrubby fields and townsites.

## Similar Birds

Eastern Bluebird          Belted Kingfisher (p. 98)

blue head
crest

black bill

blue
upperparts

white
underparts

*adult*

dark bars and
white tip
on blue tail

**Nesting:** in a tree or tall shrub; pair builds a bulky
stick nest; greenish, buff or pale eggs, spotted with
grey, olive and brown, are 28 x 20 mm; pair
incubates 4–5 eggs for 16–18 days.

### Did You Know?

Blue Jays store food from
feeders in trees and other
places for later use.

### Look For

The Blue Jay is found in
cities and towns, particularly
Edmonton and Red Deer. It
has expanded its range west-
ward because of feeders, landfills and forest fragmentation.

# Black-billed Magpie
*Pica hudsonia*

Truly among North America's most beautiful birds, Black-billed Magpies are too often discredited because of their aggressive demeanor. While many westerners consider magpies a nuisance, eastern visitors to our region are often captivated by their beauty and approachability. •-The magpie is one of the most exceptional architects among birds. Its elaborate nest is constructed of sticks and held together with mud. A domed compartment conceals and protects the eggs and young from harsh weather and predators. Abandoned nests remain in trees for years and are often used by other birds.

**Other ID:** black head, breast and back; rounded, black-and-white wings; black undertail coverts.
**Size:** *L* 46 cm; *W* 64 cm.
**Voice:** loud, nasal, frequently repeated *ueh-ueh-ueh;* also many other vocalizations.
**Status:** very common year-round.
**Habitat:** open forests, agricultural areas, riparian thickets, townsites and campgrounds.

## Similar Birds

American Crow (p. 120)

Common Raven (p. 122)

black bill

long, black tail

white belly

*adult*

**Nesting:** in a tree or tall shrub; domed stick and twig nest is often held together with mud; spotted greenish blue or olive eggs are 33 x 23 mm; female incubates 5–8 eggs for up to 24 days.

## Did You Know?

Magpies raised in captivity may learn to imitate the human voice. Some even learned to "count" or tell apart different sized groups of objects.

## Look For

Albino magpies occasionally occur with white bellies and light grey body feathers instead of black.

# American Crow
*Corvus brachyrhynchos*

The noise that emanates from this treetop squawker is not representative of its intelligence. These wary, clever birds are impressive mimics, able to whine like a dog and laugh or cry like a human. • Crows are family-oriented, and the young from the previous year help their parents to raise the next year's nestlings. • American Crows are ecological generalists, able to adapt to a variety of habitats. • Their diets are as variable, consisting of carrion, other bird's eggs and nestlings, seeds, berries and human food waste. *Corvus brachyrhynchos* is Latin for "raven with the small nose."

**Other ID:** slim, sleek head and throat.
**Size:** *L* 43–53 cm; *W* 94 cm.
**Voice:** distinctive, far-carrying, repetitive *caw-caw-caw.*
**Status:** very common migrant and breeder; a few remain throughout winter.
**Habitat:** urban areas, agricultural fields and other open areas with scattered woodlands, marshes, lakes and rivers in densely forested areas.

## Similar Birds

Common Raven (p. 122)

Black-billed Magpie (p. 118)

square-shaped tail

black bill

glossy, purple black plumage

black legs

*adult*

**Nesting:** in a coniferous or deciduous tree or on a utility pole; large stick-and-branch nest is lined with fur and soft plant materials; darkly blotched, grey green to blue green eggs are 41 x 29 mm; female incubates 4–6 eggs for about 18 days.

## Did You Know?

American Crows group together in fall in large flocks known as "murders."

## Look For

Crows and ravens are similar in appearance. To distinguish them, look for the crow's squared tail and slim beak and the raven's wedge-shaped tail and heavier bill.

# Common Raven
*Corvus corax*

The Common Raven soars with a wingspan comparable to that of hawk's, travelling along coastlines, over deserts, along mountain ridges and even on the arctic tundra. Few birds occupy such a large natural range. • The courtship performance of a Common Raven pair sends them tumbling through the air together, talons locked. Like crows, ravens are intelligent members of the corvid family and they maintain loyal, lifelong pair bonds.

**Other ID:** *In flight:* rough diamond shape to tail; soars and performs acrobatics.
**Size:** *L* 61 cm; *W* 1.3 m.
**Voice:** deep, guttural, far-carrying, repetitive *craww-craww* or *quork quork* among other vocalizations.
**Status:** uncommon to common year-round resident.
**Habitat:** coniferous and mixed forests and woodlands; townsites, campgrounds and landfills.

## Similar Birds

American Crow (p. 120)

## Look For

Sometimes you will see ravens working as a pair to confiscate a meal. One raven acts as the decoy, while the other steals the food!

black upperparts

rounded wings

heavy, black bill

shaggy throat

all-black plumage

*adult*

wedge-shaped tail

**Nesting:** on a ledge, bluff or utility pole or in a tall coniferous tree; large stick-and-branch nest is lined with fur and soft plant materials; variably marked, greenish eggs are 50 x 33 mm; female incubates 4–6 eggs for 18–21 days.

## Did You Know?

Ravens are the largest of the passerines and have been known to live up to 40 years. Native American cultures hold this bird in high regard, deeming the Common Raven the creator of the earth, moon, sun and stars, but it is also representative of a trickster figure.

# Horned Lark
*Eremophila alpestris*

An impressive, high-speed, plummeting courtship dive would blow anybody's hair back, or in the case of the Horned Lark, its two unique black horns. Long before the snow is gone, this bird's tinkling song is one of the first introductions to spring.
• Horned Larks are often abundant at roadsides, searching for seeds, but an approaching vehicle usually sends them flying into an adjacent field, making it difficult to identify them. When these birds visit in winter, you can spot them in farmers' fields or catch them at the beach visiting with Snow Buntings and Lapland Longspurs.

**Other ID:** *Female:* duller plumage.
**Size:** *L* 18 cm; *W* 30 cm.
**Voice:** call is a tinkling *tsee-titi* or *zoot;* flight song is a long series of tinkling, twittered whistles.
**Status:** common migrant and breeder; a few overwinter in southern Alberta.
**Habitat:** *Breeding:* open areas, including pastures, croplands, airfields and alpine tundra. *In migration* and *winter:* croplands, roadside ditches and fields.

## Similar Birds

Snow Bunting

Lapland Longspur

American Pipit

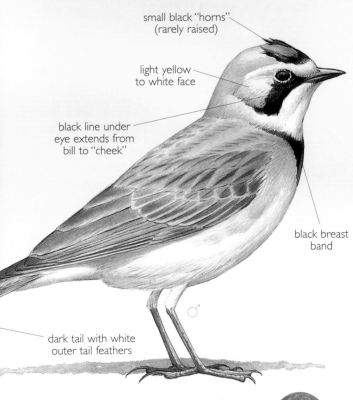

small black "horns" (rarely raised)

light yellow to white face

black line under eye extends from bill to "cheek"

black breast band

dark tail with white outer tail feathers

**Nesting:** on the ground; in a shallow scrape lined with grass, plant fibres and roots; brown-blotched, grey to greenish white eggs are 23 x 16 mm; female incubates 3–4 eggs for 10–12 days.

### Did You Know?

One way to distinguish a sparrow from a Horned Lark is by its method of travel: Horned Larks walk, while sparrows hop.

### Look For

The Horned Lark's dark tail contrasts with its light brown body and belly. This field mark will help you spot these birds in their open-country habitat.

# Tree Swallow
*Tachycineta bicolor*

Tree Swallows, our most common summer swallows, are often seen perched beside their fence post nest boxes. When conditions are favourable, these busy birds will return to their young 10 to 20 times per hour, about 140 to 300 times a day! This nearly ceaseless activity provides observers with plenty of opportunities to watch and photograph these birds in action. • In the evening and during light rains, small groups of foraging Tree Swallows sail gracefully above rivers and wetlands, catching stoneflies, mayflies and caddisflies.

**Other ID:** dark rump. *Female:* slightly duller. *Immature:* brown upperparts; white underparts.
**Size:** *L* 14 cm; *W* 37 cm.
**Voice:** alarm call is a metallic, buzzy *klweet*.
*Male:* song is a liquid, chattering twitter.
**Status:** common spring migrant and breeder.
**Habitat:** open areas, such as beaver ponds, marshes, lakeshores, field fencelines, townsites and open woodlands.

## Similar Birds

Purple Martin        Eastern Kingbird        Bank Swallow        Barn Swallow
                       (p. 108)                                        (p. 128)

iridescent, dark blue or green head and upperparts

small bill

long, pointed wings

white underparts

*adult*

shallowly forked tail

**Nesting:** in a tree cavity or nest box lined with weeds, grass and feathers; white eggs are 19 x 13 mm; female incubates 4–6 eggs for up to 19 days.

### Did You Know?

When Tree Swallows leave their nest to forage, they often cover their eggs with feathers.

### Look For

In the sunlight, the back of the Tree Swallow appears blue; in autumn migration the back appears green.

# Barn Swallow
*Hirundo rustica*

In an encounter with this bird, you might first notice its distinctive, deeply forked tail—or you might find yourself repeatedly ducking to avoid the dives of a protective parent. Barn Swallows once nested on cliffs, but they are now found more frequently nesting on human-made structures. Barns, boat-houses and areas under bridges and house eaves all provide shelter from predators and inclement weather. The messy young and aggressive parents unfortunately often motivate people to remove nests just as nesting season is beginning, but this bird's close association with humans allows us to observe the normally secretive reproductive cycle of birds.

**Other ID:** blue black upperparts; long, pointed wings.
**Size:** *L* 18 cm; *W* 38 cm.
**Voice:** continuous, twittering chatter: *zip-zip-zip* or *kvick-kvick.*
**Status:** common spring migrant and breeder.
**Habitat:** open rural and urban areas where bridges, culverts and buildings are found near water.

## Similar Birds

Cliff Swallow

Purple Martin

Tree Swallow (p. 126)

rufous throat
and forehead

rust- to buff-coloured
underparts

long, deeply
forked tail

*adult*

**Nesting:** singly or in small, loose colonies; on a human-made structure under an overhang; half or full cup nest is made of mud, grass and straw; brown-spotted, white eggs are 20 x 14 mm; pair incubates 4–7 eggs for 13–17 days.

### Did You Know?

The Barn Swallow is a natural pest controller, feeding on insects that are often harmful to crops and livestock.

### Look For

Barn Swallows roll mud into small balls and build their nests one mouthful of mud at a time.

# Black-capped Chickadee
*Poecile atricapillus*

You can catch a glimpse of this incredibly sociable chickadee at any time of the year in Alberta. In winter, Black-caps feed with kinglets, nuthatches, creepers and small woodpeckers; in spring and fall, they join mixed flocks of vireos and warblers. While observing their antics at feeders, you may even be able to entice a Black-capped Chickadee to the palm of your hand with the help of a sunflower seed. • On cold nights, chickadees enter into a hypothermic state, lowering their body temperatures and heartbeats considerably to conserve energy.

**Other ID:** black "bib"; dark legs; light buff sides and flanks.
**Size:** *L* 13–15 cm; *W* 20 cm.
**Voice:** call is a chipper, whistled *chick-a-dee-dee-dee;* song is a slow, whistled *swee-tee* or *fee-bee.*
**Status:** common to very common year-round resident.
**Habitat:** deciduous and mixed forests, riparian woodlands, wooded urban parks; backyard feeders.

## Similar Birds

Boreal Chickadee

Blackpoll Warbler

black "cap"

white "cheek"

grey back
and wings

white edging on
wing feathers

white
underparts

*adult*

**Nesting:** pair excavates a cavity in a rotting tree or stump; cavity is lined with fur, feathers, moss, grass and cocoons; occasionally uses a birdhouse; finely speckled, white eggs are 15 x 12 mm; female incubates 6–8 eggs for 12–13 days.

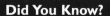

## Did You Know?

Black-capped Chickadees are thought to possess amazing memories. They can relocate seed caches up to a month after they are hidden!

## Look For

This bird sometimes feeds while hanging upside down, allowing it to grab a meal that another bird may not be able to reach.

# Red-breasted Nuthatch

*Sitta canadensis*

The Red-breasted Nuthatch may look a little like a woodpecker, but its view of the world could be considered somewhat dizzying. This interesting bird, with its distinctive black eye line and red breast, moves down tree trunks headfirst, cleaning up the seeds, insects and nuts that woodpeckers may have overlooked. • The odd name "nuthatch" comes from this bird's habit of wedging large nuts into crevices, then using its bill to hammer the nuts open. • Its species name, *canadensis,* means "of Canada."

**Other ID:** white "cheek"; black "cap"; straight bill; short tail. *Male:* black crown; deeper rust on breast. *Female:* light red wash on breast.
**Size:** *L* 11 cm; *W* 21 cm.
**Voice:** call is a slow, repeated, nasal *yank yank yank;* also a short *tsip.*
**Status:** common year-round resident.
**Habitat:** *Breeding:* spruce–fir and pine forests; pine plantations. *In migration* and *winter:* mixed woodlands, especially those near bird feeders.

## Similar Birds

White-breasted
Nuthatch

## Look For

The Red-breasted Nuthatch visits feeders, but you may only catch a glimpse of its red belly before it grabs a seed and darts away to eat it in private.

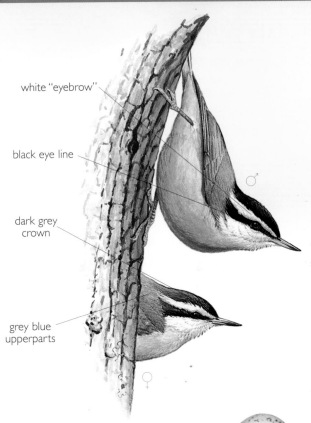

white "eyebrow"

black eye line

dark grey
crown

grey blue
upperparts

♂

♀

**Nesting:** excavates a cavity or uses an abandoned
woodpecker nest; nest is made of bark shreds,
grass and fur with sap spread at entrance; brown-
spotted, white eggs are 15 x 12 mm; female
incubates 5–6 eggs for about 12 days.

## Did You Know?

Red-breasted Nuthatches smear the entrance of their nest
cavities with sap from pine and spruce trees to keep ants
and other insects away; these creatures can transmit fungal
infections or parasitize nestlings.

# Brown Creeper
*Certhia americana*

The cryptic Brown Creeper is never easy to find, and often goes unnoticed until a flake of bark suddenly takes the shape of a bird. A frightened creeper will freeze and flatten itself against a tree trunk, becoming nearly invisible. • The Brown Creeper uses its long, stiff tail feathers to prop itself up while climbing tree trunks. When it reaches the upper branches, it floats down to the base of a neighbouring tree to begin another foraging ascent. As well as eating caterpillars and spiders, the Brown Creeper also visits suet feeders.

**Other ID:** brown back with buffy white streaks; rufous rump.
**Size:** *L* 13 cm; *W* 19 cm.
**Voice:** song is a faint, high-pitched *trees-trees-trees see the trees;* call is a high *tseee.*
**Status:** uncommon year-round resident.
**Habitat:** mature deciduous, coniferous and mixed forests and woodlands, especially in wet areas with large, dead trees; also found near bogs.

## Similar Birds

Common Nighthawk
(p. 94)

Red-breasted
Nuthatch (p. 132)

Northern Flicker
(p. 102)

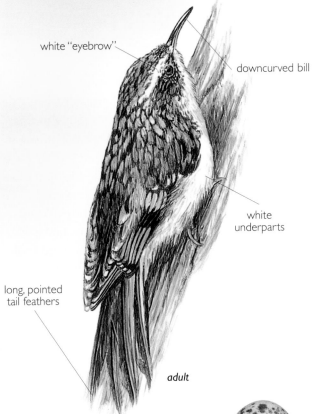

white "eyebrow"

downcurved bill

white underparts

long, pointed tail feathers

*adult*

**Nesting:** under loose bark; nest of grass and conifer needles is woven together with spider silk; brown-spotted, whitish eggs are 15 x 12 mm; female incubates 5–6 eggs for 14–17 days.

## Did You Know?

There are many species of creepers in Europe and Asia, but the Brown Creeper is the only member of its family found in North America.

## Look For

The Brown Creeper feeds by slowly spiralling up a tree trunk, searching for hidden invertebrates.

# House Wren
*Troglodytes aedon*

You might overlook the bland, nondescript plumage of this suburban and city park dweller when you hear it sing a seemingly unending song in one breath. The voice of a House Wren is as sweet as that of a nightingale. • Despite their bubbly warble, House Wrens can be very aggressive toward other species that nest in their territory. They might even puncture and toss eggs from other birds' nests. • House Wrens often build numerous nests, which later serve as decoys or "dummy" nests to fool would-be enemies.

**Other ID:** brown upperparts; fine, dark barring on upper wings and lower back; faintly barred flanks.
**Size:** *L* 12 cm; *W* 15 cm.
**Voice:** smooth, running, bubbly warble: *tsi-tsi-tsi-tsi oodle-oodle-oodle-oodle*.
**Status:** uncommon to common migrant and breeder.
**Habitat:** thickets and shrubby openings in or at the edge of deciduous or mixed woodlands; often in shrubs and thickets near buildings.

## Similar Birds

Winter Wren

Sedge Wren

short, upraised tail finely
barred with black

faint, pale "eyebrow"
and eye ring

whitish throat

whitish to buff
underparts

*adult*

**Nesting:** in a natural or artificial cavity or
abandoned woodpecker nest; nest of sticks and
grass is lined with feathers and fur; heavily marked,
white to pinkish white eggs are 16 x 13 mm;
female incubates 6–8 eggs for 12–15 days.

## Did You Know?

This bird has the largest
range of any New World
passerine, stretching from
Canada to southern South
America.

## Look For

The House Wren usually
carries its short, finely barred
tail tilted upward.

# Ruby-crowned Kinglet

*Regulus calendula*

Not only does the male Ruby-crowned Kinglet possess a loud, complex, warbling song to bring him some attention, he also wears a nifty red "mohawk" to help attract a mate and defend his territory in spring. Unfortunately, the distinctive crown of the Ruby-crowned Kinglet is only visible in breeding season, leaving the bird to wear its dull olive green plumage for the rest of the year.

**Other ID:** olive green upperparts; dark wings; flicks its wings. *Female:* lacks red crown.
**Size:** *L* 10 cm; *W* 19 cm.
**Voice:** *Male:* song is an accelerating and rising *tea-tea-tea-tew-tew-tew look-at-me, look-at-me, look-at-me.*
**Status:** common migrant and breeder.
**Habitat:** mixed woodlands and pure coniferous forests, especially with spruce; often near wet forest openings and edges.

## Similar Birds

Golden-crowned Kinglet

Orange-crowned Warbler

Yellow-bellied Flycatcher

2 bold, white
wing bars

small, red crown
usually hidden

♀

short, dark tail

bold, broken
eye ring

♂

whitish to
yellowish
underparts

**Nesting:** usually in a conifer; female builds hanging nest of lichen, twigs and leaves; brown-spotted, white to pale buff eggs are 14 x 11 mm; female incubates 7–8 eggs for 13–14 days.

## Did You Know?

Females can lay an impressively large clutch with up to 12 eggs, which together often weigh as much as the bird!

## Look For

Watch for this bird's hovering technique and wing-flicking behaviour to distinguish it from similar-looking flycatcher species.

# Mountain Bluebird
*Sialia currucoides*

Vibrant Mountain Bluebirds look like a piece of sky come to life. They perch on wire fences and tall grasses, alighting to snatch up insects on the ground or hovering briefly to pluck at berries. • Natural nest sites, such as woodpecker cavities or holes in sandstone cliffs, are in high demand. Habitat loss and increased competition with aggressive European Starlings for these sites have forced many bluebirds to nest in artificial nest boxes. A growing number of volunteer-monitored "bluebird trails" encourage bluebirds to breed in our region's rural areas.

**Other ID:** upperparts are darker than the underparts. *Female:* sky blue wings, tail and rump; grey and rufous underparts.
**Size:** *L* 18 cm; *W* 36 cm.
**Voice:** call is a low *turr turr;* male's song is a short warble of churs.
**Status:** uncommon to common migrant and breeder.
**Habitat:** *Breeding:* open and broken subalpine forests from 1200–3600 m. *In migration:* open forests and forest edges, burned forests, agricultural areas and grasslands.

## Similar Birds

Townsend's Solitaire

Blue Jay (p. 116)

blue grey back
and head

black eyes
and bill

♀

♂

sky blue
body

black legs

**Nesting:** in an abandoned woodpecker cavity,
natural cavity or nest box; cavity is lined with
plant stems, grass, conifer needles, twigs and
feathers; pale blue eggs are 22 x 17 mm; female
incubates 5–6 eggs for 13 days.

## Did You Know?

Mountain Bluebirds often
raise two broods per year,
and the fledglings may help
to gather food for the
occupants of the second
nest.

## Look For

Recently burned areas attract
bluebirds because of the
number of abandoned wood-
pecker cavities and snags.

# American Robin
*Turdus migratorius*

Come March, the familiar song of the American Robin may wake you early if you are a light sleeper. This abundant bird adapts easily to urban areas and often works from dawn until after dusk when there is a nest to be built or hungry, young mouths to feed. • The robin's bright red belly contrasted with its dark head and wings make this bird easy to identify even for a nonbirder. • Open water springs and fermenting fruit convince more and more robins to stay the winter in Alberta each year.

**Other ID:** white throat is streaked with black; black-tipped, yellow bill. *Female:* dark grey head; grey brown back.
**Size:** L 25 cm; W 43 cm.
**Voice:** song is an evenly spaced warble: *cheerily cheer-up cheerio;* call is a rapid *tut-tut-tut.*
**Status:** abundant migrant and breeder; a few birds overwinter.
**Habitat:** residential lawns and gardens, pastures, urban parks, broken forests, bogs and river shorelines.

## Similar Birds

Varied Thrush

## Look For

A hunting robin with its head tilted to the side isn't listening for prey, but is rather looking for movements in the soil, waiting for its next meal to come to the surface.

black head

incomplete
white eye ring

light red
orange breast

♂

♀

white undertail
coverts

deep brick red
breast

**Nesting:** in a coniferous or deciduous tree or
shrub; cup nest is built of grass, moss, bark and
mud; light blue eggs are 28 x 20 mm; female
incubates 4 eggs for 11–16 days.

## Did You Know?

American Robins do not use nest boxes, but prefer platforms
for their nests. The female stays busy raising up to three
broods a year and her young are easily distinguishable with
their dishevelled plumage and heavily spotted underparts.

# Gray Catbird
*Dumetella carolinensis*

This accomplished mimic may have you fooled if you hear it shuffling through underbrush and dense riparian shrubs, calling its catlike *meow*. The Gray Catbird's ability to use both sides of its syrinx allows it to sing two notes at once. • In a competitive nesting habitat of sparrows, robins and cowbirds, the Gray Catbird vigilantly defends its territory. It will destroy the eggs and nestlings of other songbirds and when approached will take on an intense defensive posture, screaming and even attempting to hit an intruder.

**Other ID:** dark grey overall; black eyes, bill and legs.
**Size:** *L* 11–14 cm; *W* 28 cm.
**Voice:** calls include a catlike *meoww* and a harsh *check-check;* song is a variety of warbles, squeaks and mimicked phrases interspersed with a *mew* call.
**Status:** uncommon to common migrant and breeder.
**Habitat:** dense thickets, brambles, shrubby or brushy areas and hedgerows, often near water.

## Similar Birds

Northern Mockingbird

Gray Jay (p. 114)

Townsend's Solitaire

black "cap"

long tail is dark grey to black

chestnut undertail coverts

*adult*

**Nesting:** in a dense shrub or thicket; bulky cup nest is made of twigs, leaves and grass; greenish blue eggs are 23 x 17 mm; female incubates 4 eggs for 12–15 days.

## Did You Know?

The watchful female Gray Catbird can recognize a Brown-headed Cowbird (p. 173) egg and will remove it from her nest.

## Look For

If you are lucky enough to see this bird during breeding season, watch the male raise his long slender tail to show off his rust-coloured undertail coverts.

# Brown Thrasher
*Toxostoma rufum*

The Brown Thrasher shares the streaked breast
of a thrush and the long tail of a catbird, but it
has a temper all its own. Because this bird nests
close to the ground, the
Brown Thrasher defends
its nest with a vengeance,

attacking snakes and other nest robbers sometimes
to the point of drawing blood. • In spite of this bird's
size, the Brown Thrasher can be hard to find in its
shrubby understorey habitat. Without a bit of coaxing
to lure it out into the open, you might only catch a
flash of the Brown Thrasher's rufous colour as it flies
from one thicket to another.

**Other ID:** orange yellow eyes; 2 white wing bars.
**Size:** *L* 22 cm; *W* 33 cm.
**Voice:** songs vary, with each phrase usually repeated
twice: *dig-it dig-it, hoe-it hoe-it, pull-it-up pull-it-up;*
calls include a loud crackling note, a harsh *shuck,*
a soft *churr* or a whistled, 3-note *pit-cher-ee.*
**Status:** uncommon to common migrant and
breeder.
**Habitat:** dense shrubs and thickets, overgrown
pastures, woodland edges and brushy areas, rarely
close to urban areas.

## Similar Birds

Hermit Thrush

## Look For

The Brown Thrasher spends
a short time in Alberta each
year from about mid-May to
early September.

long,
downcurved bill

reddish brown
upperparts

long, rufous tail

pale underparts with
heavy, brown streaking

*adult*

**Nesting:** usually in a low shrub; often on the ground; cup nest made of grass, twigs and leaves lined with vegetation; pale blue eggs, dotted with reddish brown, are 26 x 19 mm; pair incubates 4 eggs for 11–14 days.

## Did You Know?

The male Brown Thrasher has the most extensive vocal repertoire of any North American songbird. Its tune has up to 3000 combinations and twice repeated phrases with complex choruses.

# European Starling
*Sturnus vulgaris*

The European Starling did not hesitate to make itself known across North America after being released in New York's Central Park in 1890 and 1891. These highly adaptable birds not only took over the nesting sites of native cavity nesters, such as Tree Swallows and Red-headed Woodpeckers, but they learned to mimic the sounds of Killdeers, Red-tailed Hawks, Soras and meadowlarks. • Look for massive evening roosts of European Starlings under bridges or on buildings. • These birds have a variable diet consisting of Japanese beetles and other destructive agricultural pests, berries, grains and even human food waste.

**Other ID:** dark eyes; short, squared tail.
**Size:** *L* 22 cm; *W* 40 cm.
**Voice:** variety of whistles, squeaks, and gurgles; imitates other birds.
**Status:** common migrant and breeder; individuals often overwinter.
**Habitat:** agricultural areas, townsites, woodland edges, landfills and roadsides.

## Similar Birds

Rusty Blackbird

Brown-headed Cowbird (p. 172)

Brewer's Blackbird

iridescent, purple black head and neck

glossy, green back with buffy spots

yellow bill

greenish black underparts

*breeding*

**Nesting:** in an abandoned woodpecker cavity, natural cavity or nest box; nest is made of grass, twigs and straw; bluish to greenish white eggs are 30 x 21 mm; female incubates 4–6 eggs for 12–14 days.

## Did You Know?

This bird was brought to New York as part of the Shakespeare society's plan to introduce all the birds mentioned in their favourite author's writings.

## Look For

The European Starling looks somewhat like a blackbird. Look for the starling's comparably shorter tail and bright yellow bill to help you accurately identify it.

# Cedar Waxwing
*Bombycilla cedrorum*

With its black "mask" and slick hairdo, the Cedar Waxwing has a heroic look. This bird's splendid personality is reflected in its amusing antics after gorging on fermented berries and in its gentle courtship dance. To court a mate, the gentlemanly male hops toward a female and offers her a berry. The female accepts the berry and hops away, then stops, and hops back toward the male to offer him the berry in return. • Cedar Waxwings are among the last birds to nest in Alberta.

**Other ID:** brown upperparts; grey rump; yellow terminal tail band. *Juvenile:* no "mask"; streaked underparts; grey brown body.
**Size:** *L* 18 cm; *W* 30 cm.
**Voice:** faint, high-pitched, trilled whistle: *tseee-tseee-tseee.*
**Status:** uncommon to common migrant and breeder; a few overwinter.
**Habitat:** wooded residential parks and gardens, overgrown fields, forest edges, second-growth, riparian and open woodlands.

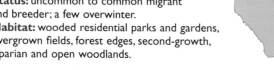

## Similar Birds

Bohemian Waxwing

## Look For

The Bohemian Waxwing is a cousin of the Cedar Waxwing, but it wanders and nests farther north in the province and is a year-round resident.

cinnamon crest

black "mask"

small red "drops" on wings

yellow wash on belly

white undertail coverts

*adult*

**Nesting:** in a coniferous or deciduous tree or shrub; cup nest is made of twigs, moss and lichen; darkly spotted, bluish to greyish eggs are 22 x 16 mm; female incubates 3–5 eggs for 12–16 days.

## Did You Know?

The yellow tail band and "waxy" red wing tips of the Cedar Waxwing get their colour from pigments in the berries that these birds eat.

# Yellow Warbler
*Dendroica petechia*

The Yellow Warbler is often parasitized by the Brown-headed Cowbird and can recognize cowbird eggs, but rather than tossing them out, it will build another nest overtop the old eggs or abandon the first nest completely. Occasionally, cowbirds strike repeatedly—a stack of five warbler nests was once found! • The widely distributed, bright Yellow Warbler arrives in May, singing its *sweet-sweet* song and is often mistakenly thought to be a "wild canary." • The Yellow Warbler flits from branch to branch in search of juicy caterpillars, aphids and beetles.

**Other ID:** yellowish legs; bright yellow highlights on dark yellow olive tail and wings.
**Size:** *L* 13 cm; *W* 20 cm.
**Voice:** song is a fast, frequently repeated *sweet-sweet-sweet summer sweet.*
**Status:** very common migrant and breeder.
**Habitat:** moist, open woodlands with dense, low scrub; shrubby meadows, willow tangles, shrubby fencerows and riparian woodlands; usually near water.

## Similar Birds

Orange-crowned
Warbler

American
Goldfinch

Common
Yellowthroat (p. 154)

Wilson's
Warbler

black bill and eyes

bright yellow body

♀

faint, red breast streaks

♂

red breast streaks

*breeding*

**Nesting:** in a deciduous tree or shrub; female builds a cup nest of grass, weeds and shredded bark; darkly speckled, greyish or greenish white eggs are 17 x 13 mm; female incubates eggs for 11–12 days.

### Did You Know?

Found throughout North America and on Central and South American islands, the Yellow Warbler has an amazing geographical range for a small bird.

### Look For

In fall migration, when male Yellow Warblers no longer wear their breeding plumage, look for flashes of yellow on the sides of their tails to distinguish them.

# Common Yellowthroat

*Geothlypis trichas*

The bumblebee colours of the male Common Yellowthroat help to identify this skulking wetland resident. The cattail outposts on which he perches to sing his *witchety* song are strategically chosen, and he visits them in rotation, fiercely guarding his territory against the intrusion of other males.
• The Common Yellowthroat is different than most wood-warblers, preferring marshlands and wet, overgrown meadows to forests. The female wears no "mask" and remains mostly hidden from view in thick vegetation where she tends to the nest.

**Other ID:** yellow undertail coverts; dingy white belly; orangy legs. *Male:* bright yellow throat and breast.
**Size:** *L* 11–14 cm; *W* 17 cm.
**Voice:** song is a clear, oscillating *witchety witchety witchety-witch;* call is a sharp *tcheck* or *tchet.*
**Status:** common migrant and breeder.
**Habitat:** cattail marshes, sedge wetlands, riparian areas, beaver ponds and wet, overgrown meadows; sometimes dry fields.

## Similar Birds

Kentucky Warbler

Wilson's Warbler

Nashville Warbler

no "mask"

may show faint, white eye ring

olive green to olive brown upperparts

♀

broad, black "mask" with white upper border

♂

**Nesting:** on or near the ground or in a small shrub or emergent vegetation; female builds an open cup nest of weeds, grass, bark strips and moss; white eggs with dark markings are 17 x 13 mm; female incubates 3–5 eggs for 12 days.

## Did You Know?

This bird is one of the most widespread warblers in Alberta. Its undulating song is a trademark sound of the province's wetlands.

## Look For

Common Yellowthroats migrate to Alberta in May and leave in September to travel to their southern wintering grounds.

# Western Tanager
*Piranga ludoviciana*

The Western Tanager brings the colours of a ripening tropical fruit to our province, but only for a short time. It raises a new generation of young and takes advantage of the seasonal explosion of food in our forests before heading back to its exotic wintering grounds in Mexico and Central America. Despite the male's stunning plumage accentuated by black wings and a black tail, the Western Tanager might take some patience to spot. • His song can also be a challenge to recognize. It resembles the robin's tune, but the Western Tanager sings it with what sounds like a sore throat.

**Other ID:** *Breeding male:* black back, wings and tail; yellow rump. *Breeding female:* duller underparts and upperparts compared to male.
**Size:** L 18 cm; 29 cm.
**Voice:** call is a hiccupy *pit-a-tik. Male:* song is hoarse and robinlike: *hurry, scurry, scurry, hurry.*
**Status:** common migrant and breeder.
**Habitat:** mature coniferous or mixedwood forests and aspen woodlands.

## Similar Birds

Baltimore Oriole (p. 174)

## Look For

Add some fresh fruit, particularly orange halves, to your bird feeder and you might attract a visiting Western Tanager.

olive green overall

♀

red forehead or entire head (variable)

light-coloured bill

faint wing bars

♂

yellow underparts and wing bars

*breeding*

**Nesting:** on a horizontal branch or fork in a conifer; cup nest is loosely built of twigs, grass and other plant materials and lined with fine vegetation; brown-spotted, light blue or greenish eggs are 23 x 17 mm; female incubates 4 eggs for 13–14 days.

## Did You Know?

The roots of the tanager family extend into the Amazon rain forest. "Tanager" is derived from *tangara,* the Tupi Indian name for this group of birds.

# Chipping Sparrow
*Spizella passerina*

Though you may spot the relatively tame Chipping Sparrow singing from a high perch, it commonly nests at eye level for birders, so this bird's breeding and nest-building rituals can be easily observed. You can take part in building this bird's nest by leaving samples of your pet's hair—or your own—around your backyard. • This bird's song resembles that of the Dark-eyed Junco. Listen for a slightly faster, drier and less musical series of notes to identify the Chipping Sparrow.

**Other ID:** dark bill; light grey, unstreaked under-parts. *Nonbreeding:* paler crown with dark streaks; brown "eyebrow" and "cheek"; pale lower mandible.
**Size:** *L* 13–15 cm; *W* 21 cm.
**Voice:** song is a rapid, dry trill of *chip* notes; call is a high-pitched *chip*.
**Status:** very common migrant and breeder.
**Habitat:** open conifers or mixed woodland edges; yards and gardens with tree and shrub borders.

## Similar Birds

American Tree Sparrow        Swamp Sparrow

prominent rufous "cap"

white "eyebrow"

black eye line

mottled brown
upperparts

*breeding*

**Nesting:** usually at midlevel in a coniferous tree; female builds a cup nest of grass and rootlets lined with hair; pale blue, sparsely marked eggs are 18 x 13 mm; female incubates 4 eggs for 11–12 days.

## Did You Know?

The Chipping Sparrow is the most common and widely distributed migrating sparrow in North America.

## Look For

Chipping Sparrows visit feeders and forage on lawns for the seeds of grass, dandelions and clovers.

# Song Sparrow
*Melospiza melodia*

Although its plumage is unremarkable, the appropriately named Song Sparrow is among the great singers of the bird world. By the time a young male Song Sparrow is a few months old, he has created a courtship tune of his own, having learned the basics of melody and rhythm from his father and male rivals. • In breeding season, pairs of Song Sparrows raise as many as three or four families. The presence of a well-stocked backyard feeder may be a fair trade for a sweet song in the dead of winter.

**Other ID:** white jaw line; dark eye line on greyish face; mottled brown upperparts; rounded tail tip.
**Size:** L 14–18 cm; W 20 cm.
**Voice:** song is 1–4 introductory notes, such as *sweet sweet sweet,* followed by buzzy *towee,* then a short, descending trill; call is short *tsip* or *tchep.*
**Status:** very common migrant and breeder; a few might overwinter.
**Habitat:** willow shrublands, riparian thickets, forest openings and pastures, all often near water.

## Similar Birds

Lincoln's Sparrow

Fox Sparrow

Savannah Sparrow

dark crown with pale central stripe

dark "moustache" stripes

heavy brown streaks converge at central breast spot

*adult*

**Nesting:** usually on the ground or in a low shrub; female builds an open cup nest of grass, weeds and bark strips; brown-blotched, bluish or greenish white eggs are 22 × 17 mm; female incubates 3–5 eggs for 12–14 days.

## Did You Know?

Though female songbirds are not usually vocal, the female Song Sparrow will occasionally sing a tune of her own.

## Look For

The male Song Sparrow is thought to pump his tail in flight and flutter his wings with his feet dangling, all for the purpose of attracting a mate.

# Dark-eyed Junco
*Junco hyemalis*

You might feel some sympathy for this sparrow as it picks at scraps under your backyard feeder, but the Dark-eyed Junco prefers to avoid the crowd of noshing chickadees, nuthatches and jays. In 1973, the American Ornithologists' Union grouped five junco species, all of which interbreed where their ranges meet, into a single species called the Dark-eyed Junco. Although Juncos stay around feeders past the first snowfall, most of them seem to leave the province before the Christmas bird counts.

**Other ID:** *Female:* brown overall. *Oregon Junco:* reddish brown back and flanks. *Male:* black "hood." *Female:* dark brown "hood." *Pink-sided Junco:* pink flanks; light brown back; grey head. *Northern Rockies Junco:* black "hood"; brownish back; light brown sides.
**Size:** *L* 14–17 cm; *W* 23 cm.
**Voice:** song is a long, dry trill; call is a smacking *chip* note, often given in series.
**Status:** very common migrant and breeder.
**Habitat:** *Breeding:* coniferous and mixed forests; shrubby, regenerating areas. *In migration* and *winter:* shrubby woodland borders, backyard feeders.

## Similar Birds

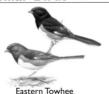

Eastern Towhee

## Look For

The Dark-eyed Junco flashes its distinctive white outer tail feathers as it rushes for cover after being flushed.

pale, conical bill

dark slate
grey overall

white outer
tail feathers

white belly
and undertail
coverts

♂

*"Slate-coloured Junco"*

**Nesting:** on the ground, usually concealed; female builds a cup nest of twigs, grass, bark shreds and moss; brown-marked, whitish to bluish eggs are 19 x 14 mm; female incubates 3–5 eggs for 12–13 days.

## Did You Know?

There are four subspecies of Dark-eyed Junco. The Slate-coloured Junco nests in the boreal forest, the Oregon Junco in the Rockies south of Jasper, the Pink-sided Junco in the Cypress Hills and the Northern Rockies Junco in Jasper National Park.

# Rose-breasted Grosbeak

*Pheucticus ludovicianus*

The Rose-breasted Grosbeak's stout, conical bill gives its head a more rounded appearance. "Gros," French for "large," certainly describes this bird's distinctive profile. Though the female lacks the formal dress of the male, she joins him in song, an unusual trait for most female songbirds. • Rose-breasted Grosbeaks often have two broods in a breeding season. Both parents incubate the eggs and occasionally sing from the nest, introducing the young to a world of melody.

**Other ID:** *Male:* black "hood" and back; thin crown stripe; brown upperparts; white rump; dark wings with small white patches. *Female:* buff underparts with dark brown streaking.
**Size:** L 18–21 cm; W 31 cm.
**Voice:** song is a long, melodious series of whistled notes, much like a fast version of a robin's song; call is a distinctive squeak.
**Status:** uncommon to common migrant and breeder.
**Habitat:** deciduous and mixed forests.

## Similar Birds

Purple Finch (p. 176)

Lark Bunting

Spotted Towhee

bold whitish "eyebrow"

pale, conical bill

♀

♂

red breast

white underparts

dark tail

**Nesting:** fairly low in a tree or tall shrub, often near water; mostly the female builds a cup nest with twigs, bark strips, grass and leaves lined with rootlets and hair; pale greenish blue eggs spotted with reddish brown are 25 x 18 mm; pair incubates 3–5 eggs for 13–14 days.

## Did You Know?

Mating grosbeaks appear pleasantly affectionate toward each other, often touching bills during courtship and after time apart.

## Look For

The Rose-breasted Grosbeak typically builds its nest low in a tree, but forages high in the canopy. You can spot it at eye level feasting on berries in fall.

# Red-winged Blackbird

*Agelaius phoeniceus*

The male Red-winged Blackbird wears his bright red shoulders like armour—together with his short, raspy song, they are key to defending his territory from rivals. In field experiments, males whose red shoulders were painted black soon lost their territories. • It isn't hard to spot the polygynous males perched on cattails in roadside ditches and wetlands, but the cryptically coloured females usually remain inconspicuous on their nests. Males arrive in Alberta for the breeding season a week or so before the females.

**Other ID:** *Female:* mottled brown upperparts; pale "eyebrow."
**Size:** *L* 18–24 cm; *W* 33 cm.
**Voice:** song is a loud, raspy *konk-a-ree* or *ogle-reeeee;* calls include a harsh *check* and high *tseert;* female gives a loud *che-che-che chee chee chee.*
**Status:** uncommon to common migrant and breeder.
**Habitat:** cattail marshes, wet meadows and ditches, croplands and shoreline shrubs.

## Similar Birds

Rusty Blackbird

Brown-headed Cowbird (p. 172)

Brewer's Blackbird

red shoulder
patch edged
in yellow

faint, red
shoulder
patch

♂

black
overall

♀

heavily
streaked
underparts

**Nesting:** colonial; in cattails or shoreline bushes; female builds an open cup nest of dried cattail leaves lined with fine grass; darkly marked, pale blue green to grey eggs are 25 x 18 mm; female incubates 3–4 eggs for 10–12 days.

## Did You Know?

Some scientists believe that the Red-winged Blackbird is the most abundant bird of any species in North America.

## Look For

Red-winged Blackbirds gather in immense flocks in agricultural areas and open fields before migrating south for the winter.

# Western Meadowlark
*Sturnella neglecta*

A lack of recognition as a separate species earned the Western Meadowlark the scientific name, *neglecta*. Distinguishing this bird from its eastern twin might be one of the more challenging identification tests of birding. With the same cryptic outfit and grassy meadow residence, there is little to tell them apart. Western Meadowlarks do, however, prefer drier, more barren grasslands compared with the wetter habitat of the Eastern Meadowlark. Their differing songs is probably the most accurate way to distinguish them.

**Other ID:** yellow lores; brown crown stripes and eye line border; pale "eyebrow" and median crown stripe; broad, black breast band; dark streaking on white sides and flanks; long, pinkish legs.
**Size:** *L* 23–24 cm; *W* 35–38 cm.
**Voice:** song is rich, melodic series of bubbly, flute-like notes; calls include a low, loud *chuck* or *chup,* a rattling flight call or a few clear whistled notes.
**Status:** common migrant and breeder.
**Habitat:** grassy meadows and pastures; also in some croplands, weedy fields and grassy roadsides.

## Similar Birds

Eastern Meadowlark

Dickcissel

long, sharp bill

mottled brown
upperparts

white outer
tail feathers

yellow underparts

*breeding*

short,
wide tail

**Nesting:** in a depression or scrape on the ground in dense grass; domed grass nest with side entrance is woven into surrounding vegetation; brown- and purple-spotted, white eggs are 28 x 21 mm; female incubates 3–7 eggs for 13–15 days.

## Did You Know?

Eastern Meadowlarks and Western Meadowlarks may occasionally interbreed where their ranges overlap, but the resulting offspring is infertile.

## Look For

Watch for the Western Meadowlark's courtship dance. Potential partners face each other, raise their bills high in the air and perform a grassland ballet.

# Yellow-headed Blackbird
*Xanthocephalus xanthocephalus*

You might be taken aback by the pitiful grinding sound that is produced when the male Yellow-headed Blackbird arches his dazzling golden head backward to sing. A nonmuscial series of grating notes leave other sounds to be desired amongst the cattails of this bird's home. • Crafty Yellow-headed Blackbirds strategically share their soggy habitat with the smaller Red-winged Blackbirds; Yellow-heads tend to command the centre of the wetland, pushing competitors to the periphery where predation is highest.

**Other ID:** *Male:* black lores; long tail; black bill. *Female:* yellow breast, throat and "eyebrow."
**Size:** L 20–28 cm; W 33–38 cm.
**Voice:** song is a strained, metallic grating note followed by a descending buzz; call is a deep *krrt* or *ktuk;* low quacks and liquidy clucks may be given during breeding season.
**Status:** common migrant and breeder.
**Habitat:** deep marshes, sloughs, lakeshores and river impoundments where cattails dominate.

## Similar Birds

Rusty Blackbird

Brewer's Blackbird

dusky brown overall

♀

yellow head and breast

white wing patches

black body

♂

**Nesting:** loosely colonial; female builds a deep basket of aquatic plants lined with dry grass, woven into surrounding vegetation over water; grey- or brown-marked, pale green to grey eggs are 26 x 18 mm; female incubates 4 eggs for 11–13 days.

## Did You Know?

The Yellow-headed Blackbird requires a hemi-marsh habitat with a 50:50 ratio of emergent vegetation and open water.

## Look For

These blackbirds often nest in small colonies of about 30 pairs. The yellow heads of the males turn fields to the colour of mustard.

# Brown-headed Cowbird
*Molothrus ater*

Brown-headed Cowbirds are best described as pests. These nomads historically followed bison herds across the prairies. They do not build their own nests, but instead lay their eggs in other birds' nests. Unsuspecting mothers are left to incubate the cowbird eggs and raise the aggressive young. Orioles, warblers, vireos and tanagers are among the most affected. • Increased livestock farming and fragmentation of forests has encouraged the expansion of the cowbird's range and it now parasitizes more than 140 bird species.

**Other ID:** dark eyes; short, squared tail. *Female:* pale throat; brown overall.
**Size:** *L* 15–20 cm; *W* 30 cm.
**Voice:** song is a high, liquidy gurgle: *glug-ahl-whee* or *bubbloozeee;* call is a squeaky, high-pitched *seep, psee* or *wee-tse-tse* or fast, chipping *ch-ch-ch-ch-ch-ch.*
**Status:** very common migrant and breeder; rare to locally common winter visitor.
**Habitat:** agricultural and residential areas, usually fields, woodland edges, utility cutlines, roadsides, fencelines, landfills, campgrounds and areas near cattle.

## Similar Birds

Brewer's Blackbird          Rusty Blackbird          Common Grackle

dark eyes

dark brown head

light brown underparts
with faint streaking ♀

thick,
conical bill

iridescent, green
blue body plumage

♂

**Nesting:** does not build a nest; female lays up to
40 eggs a year in the nests of other birds, usually
1 egg per nest; brown-speckled, whitish eggs are
21 x 16 mm; eggs hatch after 10–13 days.

## Did You Know?

In his courtship display,
the male points his bill
upward, fans his tail and
wings and utters a loud
*squeek*. No pair bond is
formed.

## Look For

When cowbirds feed in flocks,
they hold their back ends up
high, with their tails sticking
straight up in the air.

# Baltimore Oriole
*Icterus galbula*

With a robinlike song and a preference for
the canopies of your neighbourhood trees, the
Baltimore Oriole is difficult to spot, and a hanging
pouch nest dangling in a bare tree in fall is sometimes
the only evidence the bird was there at all. Orioles
spend more than half of each year in the tropics
of Central and South America, but they breed in
Alberta and across Canada. Their nests are deceptively
strong and often remain intact through the harshest
winters. • A very few of these birds stick around
in winter, and you might see one in its Halloween
colours at a feeder that offers orange halves.

**Other ID:** *Male:* black wings and central tail feathers.
*Female:* white wing bar.
**Size:** *L* 18–20 cm; *W* 29 cm.
**Voice:** song consists of slow, clear whistles: *peter
peter peter here peter;* calls include a 2-note *tea-too*
and a rapid chatter: *ch-ch-ch-ch-ch.*
**Status:** uncommon to common in spring migration
and breeding.
**Habitat:** deciduous and mixed forests, particularly
riparian woodlands, natural openings, shorelines,
roadsides, orchards, gardens and parklands.

## Similar Birds

Summer Tanager

Scarlet Tanager

olive brown
upperparts

black "hood"
and back

white wing
patch and
feather edgings

♀

♂

dull yellow
orange underparts
and rump

bright orange
underparts

**Nesting:** high in a deciduous tree; female builds a hanging pouch nest of grass, bark shreds and grapevines, occasionally adding string; darkly marked, pale grey to bluish white eggs are 23 x 15 mm; female incubates 4–5 eggs for 12–14 days.

## Did You Know?

The male Baltimore Oriole's breeding colours mirror the coat of arms of George Calvert, the Irishman who established the first colony in Maryland.

## Look For

The Baltimore Oriole has a short stay in Alberta from late May to August, although you might see a few in the winter.

# Purple Finch

*Carpodacus purpureus*

Despite its name, the Purple Finch's stunning plumage is more raspberry red than purple. Its musical *pik* call is given frequently and is a good way to know if this finch is nearby. A flat, raised, table-style feeding station and nearby tree cover are sure to attract Purple Finches, and a feeder may keep a small flock in your area over winter. • In breeding season, the male dances around the female, beating his wings rapidly until they become a blur and he gracefully lifts into the air.

**Other ID:** notched tail. *Male:* raspberry red head, throat, breast and nape; brown and red streaking on back and flanks; red rump. *Female:* white "eyebrow" and lower "cheek" stripe; grey brown upperparts with whitish streaks.
**Size:** *L* 13–15 cm; *W* 25 cm.
**Voice:** song is a bubbly, continuous warble; call is a single metallic *pik*.
**Status:** uncommon to common migrant and breeder; a few overwinter.
**Habitat:** townsites; pine, spruce and mixed forests.

## Similar Birds

House Finch

Red Crossbill

dark brown "cheek"
and "jawline"

♀

whitish
underparts
heavily streaked
with brown

pale bill

reddish brown
"cheek"

♂

pale, unstreaked
underparts

**Nesting:** on a conifer branch, far from
the trunk; female builds a cup nest of twigs, grass
and rootlets; darkly marked, pale greenish blue
eggs are 20 x 15 mm; female incubates 4–5 eggs
for 13 days.

### Did You Know?

Regular predators of the
Purple Finch include Blue
Jays, Merlins, Barn Owls
and Sharp-shinned Hawks.

### Look For

The male often delivers his
song from an exposed perch
at the top of a tree.

# White-winged Crossbill
*Loxia leucoptera*

The unique bill of the White-winged Crossbill is shared by only one other bird in North America—the Red Crossbill. Its crossed mandibles are adapted to pry open cones to eat the seeds of spruce, fir and tamarack. It also uses its strong bill as a third foot to move itself along branches. • The White-winged Crossbill is a vagrant and some years it will not visit the province at all. In winter in Alberta, adults gather in flocks at the tops of spruce trees, creating showers of conifer cone skeletons and a crackling chatter of bills. But, like many finches, they can be abundant one winter and nearly absent the next.

**Other ID:** *Female:* dusky yellow underparts slightly streaked with brown; dark wings and tail.
**Size:** L 15–17 cm; W 26 cm.
**Voice:** song is a high-pitched series of warbles, trills and chips; call is a series of harsh, questioning *cheat* notes, often given in flight.
**Status:** uncommon to common year-round.
**Habitat:** coniferous forests, primarily spruce–fir, and occasionally townsites and deciduous forests.

## Similar Birds

Red Crossbill    Pine Siskin    Pine Grosbeak    House Finch

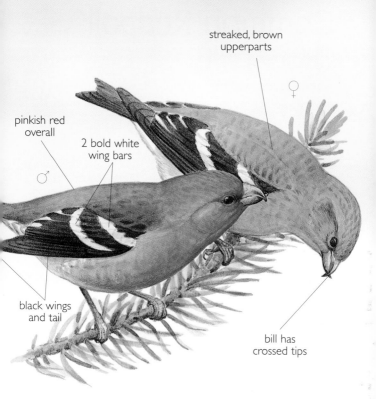

streaked, brown
upperparts

♀

pinkish red
overall

♂

2 bold white
wing bars

black wings
and tail

bill has
crossed tips

**Nesting:** on an outer branch in a conifer; female
builds an open cup nest of twigs, grass, bark shreds,
leaves and moss lined with rootlets and hair; pale
blue green eggs spotted with brown and lavender
are 21 x 15 mm; female incubates 2–4 eggs for
12–14 days.

## Did You Know?

The White-winged
Crossbill occasionally
hangs upside down from
a limb or pine cone to
feed.

## Look For

You might catch a glimpse
of White-winged Crossbills
licking the salt from winter
roads, a dangerous habit that
often results in crossbill
fatalities.

# Common Redpoll
*Carduelis flammea*

These tiny snowplows sometimes make a modest appearance, showing up in winter in Alberta in small groups of a dozen or less. Depending on the year, however, they might appear in flocks of hundreds, gleaning waste grain from bare fields or stocking up at winter feeders. • A large surface area relative to its small internal volume puts the Common Redpoll at risk of freezing in cold temperatures, but an insulating layer of warm air created by its fluffed feathers and high intake of food keep this songbird from dying of hypothermia.

**Other ID:** yellowish bill; lightly streaked sides, flanks and undertail coverts.
**Size:** *L* 13 cm; *W* 22 cm.
**Voice:** song is a twittering series of trills; calls are a soft *chit-chit-chit-chit* and a faint *swe-eet*.
**Status:** common in migration and winter.
**Habitat:** open fields and meadows; along roadsides, utility power lines, railways, forest edges; backyards with feeders.

## Similar Birds

Hoary Redpoll

Pine Siskin

Purple Finch (p. 176)

red forecrown

black "chin"

whitish to pale grey breast

♀

pinkish red breast

notched tail

♂

*nonbreeding*

**Nesting:** low in a shrub or dwarf spruce; occasionally in a grass clump; open cup nest is made of fine twigs, grass and moss; darkly speckled, pale blue eggs are 17 x 13 mm; female incubates 4–5 eggs for 12 days.

## Did You Know?

Common Redpolls spend a lot of time at feeders in the winter and prefer birch and alder seeds because of their high calorie content.

## Look For

Common Redpolls slide down snowbanks on their bellies and can endure colder temperatures than any other songbird.

# House Sparrow

*Passer domesticus*

A black "mask" and "bib" adorn the male of this adaptive, aggressive species. The House Sparrow's tendency to usurp territory has led to a decline in native bird populations. This sparrow will even help itself to the convenience of another bird's home, such as a bluebird or Cliff Swallow nest or a Purple Martin house. • This abundant and conspicuous bird was introduced to North America in the 1850s as part of a plan to control the insects that were damaging grain and cereal crops. As it turns out, these birds are largely vegetarian!

**Other ID:** *Breeding male:* light grey "cheek"; grey crown; dark, mottled upperparts; grey underparts. *Female:* indistinct facial patterns; greyish unstreaked underparts; streaked upperparts.
**Size:** *L* 14–17 cm; W 24 cm.
**Voice:** song is a plain, familiar *cheep-cheep-cheep-cheep;* call is a short *chill-up.*
**Status:** abundant year-round resident.
**Habitat:** townsites, urban and suburban areas, farmyards and agricultural areas, railway yards and other developed areas.

## Similar Birds

Harris's Sparrow

## Look For

In spring, House Sparrows feast on the buds of fruit trees. In winter, these birds flock together in barns in rural areas and at garbage dumps in cities.

buffy "eyebrow"

plain grey
brown overall

chestnut
brown nape
extends to eye

black bill

black "bib"

white wing bar

♀

♂

*breeding*

**Nesting:** often communal; in a human-made structure, ornamental shrub or natural cavity; pair builds a large dome nest of grass, twigs and plant fibres; variably marked, white to greenish eggs are 23 x 16 mm; pair incubates 4–6 eggs for 10–13 days.

## Did You Know?

House Sparrows are not closely related to the other North American sparrows, but belong to the family of Old World Sparrows or "Weaver Finches."

# Glossary

**accipiter:** a forest hawk (genus *Accipiter*), characterized by a long tail and short, rounded wings; feeds mostly on birds.

**brood:** *n.* a family of young from one hatching; *v.* to incubate the eggs.

**brood parasite:** a bird that lays its eggs in other birds' nests.

**buteo:** a high-soaring hawk (genus *Buteo*), characterized by broad wings and a short, wide tail; feeds mostly on small mammals and other land animals.

**cere:** on birds of prey, a fleshy area at the base of the bill that contains the nostrils.

**clutch:** the number of eggs laid by the female at one time.

**dabbling:** a foraging technique used by some ducks, in which the head and neck are submerged but the body and tail remain on the water's surface; dabbling ducks can usually walk easily on land, can take off without running and have brightly coloured speculums.

**"eclipse" plumage:** a cryptic plumage, similar to that of females, worn by some male ducks in autumn when they moult their flight feathers and consequently are unable to fly.

**flushing:** when frightened birds explode into flight in response to a disturbance.

**flycatching:** a feeding behaviour in which the bird leaves a perch, snatches an insect in mid-air and returns to the same perch; also known as "hawking" or "sallying."

**pelagic:** refers to birds that inhabit the ocean very far from land.

**precocial:** a bird that is relatively well developed at hatching; precocial birds usually have open eyes, extensive down and are fairly mobile.

**riparian:** refers to habitat along riverbanks.

**sexual dimorphism:** a difference in plumage, size, or other characteristics between males and females of the same species.

**speculum:** a brightly coloured patch on the wings of many dabbling ducks.

**stage:** to gather in one place during migration, usually when birds are flightless or partly flightless during moulting.

**stoop:** a steep dive through the air, usually performed by birds of prey while foraging or during courtship displays.

# Checklist

The following checklist contains 304 species of birds that are regularly seen in Alberta. Species are grouped by family and listed in taxonomic order in accordance with the A.O.U. *Check-list of North American Birds* (7th ed.) and its supplements. Rarities are noted in *italics*.

## Waterfowl
❑ Greater White-fronted Goose
❑ Snow Goose
❑ Ross's Goose
❑ Canada Goose
❑ Trumpeter Swan
❑ Tundra Swan
❑ Wood Duck
❑ Gadwall
❑ Eurasian Wigeon
❑ American Wigeon
❑ American Black Duck
❑ Mallard
❑ Blue-winged Teal
❑ Cinnamon Teal
❑ Northern Shoveler
❑ Northern Pintail
❑ Green-winged Teal
❑ Canvasback
❑ Redhead
❑ Ring-necked Duck
❑ Greater Scaup
❑ Lesser Scaup
❑ Harlequin Duck
❑ Surf Scoter
❑ White-winged Scoter
❑ Long-tailed Duck
❑ Bufflehead
❑ Common Goldeneye
❑ Barrow's Goldeneye
❑ Hooded Merganser
❑ Common Merganser
❑ Red-breasted Merganser
❑ Ruddy Duck

## Grouse & Allies
❑ Gray Partridge
❑ Ring-necked Pheasant
❑ Ruffed Grouse
❑ Greater Sage-Grouse
❑ Spruce Grouse
❑ Willow Ptarmigan
❑ White-tailed Ptarmigan
❑ Blue Grouse
❑ Sharp-tailed Grouse
❑ Wild Turkey

## Loons
❑ Red-throated Loon
❑ Pacific Loon
❑ Common Loon

## Grebes
❑ Pied-billed Grebe
❑ Horned Grebe
❑ Red-necked Grebe
❑ Eared Grebe
❑ Western Grebe
❑ Clark's Grebe

## Pelicans
❑ American White Pelican

## Cormorants
❑ Double-crested Cormorant

## Herons
❑ American Bittern
❑ Great Blue Heron
❑ *Cattle Egret*
❑ Black-crowned Night-Heron

## Ibises
❑ White Ibis

## Vultures
- ❏ Turkey Vulture

## Hawks & Eagles
- ❏ Osprey
- ❏ Bald Eagle
- ❏ Northern Harrier
- ❏ Sharp-shinned Hawk
- ❏ Cooper's Hawk
- ❏ Northern Goshawk
- ❏ Broad-winged Hawk
- ❏ Swainson's Hawk
- ❏ Red-tailed Hawk
- ❏ Ferruginous Hawk
- ❏ Rough-legged Hawk
- ❏ Golden Eagle

## Falcons
- ❏ American Kestrel
- ❏ Merlin
- ❏ Gyrfalcon
- ❏ Peregrine Falcon
- ❏ Prairie Falcon

## Rails & Coots
- ❏ Yellow Rail
- ❏ Virginia Rail
- ❏ Sora
- ❏ American Coot

## Cranes
- ❏ Sandhill Crane
- ❏ Whooping Crane

## Plovers
- ❏ Black-bellied Plover
- ❏ American Golden-Plover
- ❏ Semipalmated Plover
- ❏ Piping Plover
- ❏ Killdeer
- ❏ Mountain Plover

## Stilts & Avocets
- ❏ Black-necked Stilt
- ❏ American Avocet

## Sandpipers & Allies
- ❏ Greater Yellowlegs
- ❏ Lesser Yellowlegs
- ❏ Solitary Sandpiper
- ❏ Willet
- ❏ Spotted Sandpiper
- ❏ Upland Sandpiper
- ❏ Whimbrel
- ❏ Long-billed Curlew
- ❏ Hudsonian Godwit
- ❏ Marbled Godwit
- ❏ Ruddy Turnstone
- ❏ Red Knot
- ❏ Sanderling
- ❏ Semipalmated Sandpiper
- ❏ Western Sandpiper
- ❏ Least Sandpiper
- ❏ White-rumped Sandpiper
- ❏ Baird's Sandpiper
- ❏ Pectoral Sandpiper
- ❏ Dunlin
- ❏ Stilt Sandpiper
- ❏ Buff-breasted Sandpiper
- ❏ *Ruff*
- ❏ Short-billed Dowitcher
- ❏ Long-billed Dowitcher
- ❏ Common Snipe
- ❏ Wilson's Phalarope
- ❏ Red-necked Phalarope
- ❏ *Red Phalarope*

## Gulls & Allies
- ❏ Parasitic Jaeger
- ❏ Franklin's Gull
- ❏ Bonaparte's Gull
- ❏ Mew Gull
- ❏ Ring-billed Gull
- ❏ California Gull
- ❏ Herring Gull
- ❏ Thayer's Gull
- ❏ Glaucous Gull
- ❏ Sabine's gull
- ❏ Caspian Tern
- ❏ Common Tern
- ❏ *Arctic Tern*
- ❏ Forster's Tern
- ❏ Black Tern

## Pigeons & Doves
- ❏ Rock Dove
- ❏ Mourning Dove

## Cuckoos
- ❏ Black-billed Cuckoo

## Owls
- ❏ Great Horned Owl
- ❏ Snowy Owl
- ❏ Northern Hawk Owl
- ❏ Northern Pygmy-Owl
- ❏ Burrowing Owl
- ❏ Barred Owl
- ❏ Great Gray Owl
- ❏ Long-eared Owl
- ❏ Short-eared Owl
- ❏ Boreal Owl
- ❏ Northern Saw-whet Owl

## Nightjars
- ❏ Common Nighthawk
- ❏ *Common Poorwill*

## Swifts
- ❏ Black Swift
- ❏ Vaux's Swift

## Hummingbirds
- ❏ Ruby-throated Hummingbird
- ❏ Calliope Hummingbird
- ❏ Rufous Hummingbird

## Kingfishers
- ❏ Belted Kingfisher

## Woodpeckers
- ❏ *Red-headed Woodpecker*
- ❏ Yellow-bellied Sapsucker
- ❏ Red-naped Sapsucker
- ❏ Downy Woodpecker
- ❏ Hairy Woodpecker
- ❏ American Three-toed Woodpecker
- ❏ Black-backed Woodpecker
- ❏ Northern Flicker
- ❏ Pileated Woodpecker

## Flycatchers
- ❏ Olive-sided Flycatcher
- ❏ Western Wood-Pewee
- ❏ Yellow-bellied Flycatcher
- ❏ Alder Flycatcher
- ❏ Willow Flycatcher
- ❏ Least Flycatcher
- ❏ Hammond's Flycatcher
- ❏ Dusky Flycatcher
- ❏ Cordilleran Flycatcher
- ❏ Eastern Phoebe
- ❏ Say's Phoebe
- ❏ Great Crested Flycatcher
- ❏ Western Kingbird
- ❏ Eastern Kingbird

## Shrikes
- ❏ Loggerhead Shrike
- ❏ Northern Shrike

## Vireos
- ❏ Cassin's Vireo
- ❏ Blue-headed Vireo
- ❏ Warbling Vireo
- ❏ Philadelphia Vireo
- ❏ Red-eyed Vireo

## Jays & Crows
- ❏ Gray Jay
- ❏ Stellar's Jay
- ❏ Blue Jay
- ❏ Clark's Nutcracker
- ❏ Black-billed Magpie
- ❏ American Crow
- ❏ Common Raven

## Larks
- ❏ Horned Lark

## Swallows
- ❏ Purple Martin
- ❏ Tree Swallow
- ❏ Violet-green Swallow
- ❏ Northern Rough-winged Swallow
- ❏ Bank Swallow
- ❏ Cliff Swallow
- ❏ Barn Swallow

## Chickadees
- ❏ Black-capped Chickadee
- ❏ Mountain Chickadee
- ❏ *Chestnut-backed Chickadee*
- ❏ Boreal Chickadee

## Nuthatches
- ❏ Red-breasted Nuthatch
- ❏ White-breasted Nuthatch

## Creepers
- ❏ Brown Creeper

## Wrens
- ❏ Rock Wren
- ❏ House Wren
- ❏ Winter Wren
- ❏ Sedge Wren
- ❏ Marsh Wren

## Dippers
- ❏ American Dipper

## Kinglets
- ❏ Golden-crowned Kinglet
- ❏ Ruby-crowned Kinglet

## Thrushes
- ❏ *Eastern Bluebird*
- ❏ *Western Bluebird*
- ❏ Mountain Bluebird
- ❏ Townsend's Solitaire
- ❏ Veery
- ❏ Gray-cheeked Thrush
- ❏ Swainson's Thrush
- ❏ Hermit Thrush
- ❏ American Robin
- ❏ Varied Thrush

## Mimics & Thrashers
- ❏ Gray Catbird
- ❏ Northern Mockingbird
- ❏ *Sage Thrasher*
- ❏ Brown Thrasher

## Starlings
- ❏ European Starling

## Pipits
- ❏ American Pipit
- ❏ Sprague's Pipit

## Waxwings
- ❏ Bohemian Waxwing
- ❏ Cedar Waxwing

## Wood-Warblers
- ❏ Tennessee Warbler
- ❏ Orange-crowned Warbler
- ❏ Nashville Warbler
- ❏ Yellow Warbler
- ❏ Chestnut-sided Warbler
- ❏ Magnolia Warbler
- ❏ Cape May Warbler
- ❏ *Black-throated Blue Warbler*
- ❏ Yellow-rumped Warbler
- ❏ Black-throated Green Warbler
- ❏ Townsend's Warbler
- ❏ Blackburnian Warbler
- ❏ Palm Warbler
- ❏ Bay-breasted Warbler
- ❏ Blackpoll Warbler
- ❏ Black-and-white Warbler
- ❏ American Redstart
- ❏ Ovenbird
- ❏ Northern Waterthrush
- ❏ Connecticut Warbler
- ❏ Mourning Warbler
- ❏ MacGillivray's Warbler
- ❏ Common Yellowthroat
- ❏ Wilson's Warbler
- ❏ Canada Warbler
- ❏ Yellow-breasted Chat

## Tanagers
- ❏ Western Tanager

## Sparrows & Allies
- ❏ Spotted Towhee
- ❏ American Tree Sparrow
- ❏ Chipping Sparrow
- ❏ Clay-colored Sparrow
- ❏ Brewer's Sparrow
- ❏ Vesper Sparrow
- ❏ Lark Sparrow
- ❏ Lark Bunting
- ❏ Savannah Sparrow
- ❏ Grasshopper Sparrow
- ❏ Baird's Sparrow
- ❏ Le Conte's Sparrow
- ❏ Nelson's Sharp-tailed Sparrow
- ❏ Fox Sparrow
- ❏ Song Sparrow
- ❏ Lincoln's Sparrow

- ❏ Swamp Sparrow
- ❏ White-throated Sparrow
- ❏ Harris's Sparrow
- ❏ White-crowned Sparrow
- ❏ Golden-crowned Sparrow
- ❏ Dark-eyed Junco
- ❏ McCown's Longspur
- ❏ Lapland Longspur
- ❏ Smith's Longspur
- ❏ Chestnut-collared Longspur
- ❏ Snow Bunting

**Grosbeaks & Buntings**
- ❏ *Northern Cardinal*
- ❏ Rose-breasted Grosbeak
- ❏ Black-headed Grosbeak
- ❏ Lazuli Bunting

**Blackbirds & Allies**
- ❏ Bobolink
- ❏ Red-winged Blackbird
- ❏ Western Meadowlark
- ❏ Yellow-headed Blackbird

- ❏ Rusty Blackbird
- ❏ Brewer's Blackbird
- ❏ Common Grackle
- ❏ Brown-headed Cowbird
- ❏ Bullock's Oriole
- ❏ Baltimore Oriole

**Finches**
- ❏ Gray-crowned Rosy Finch
- ❏ Pine Grosbeak
- ❏ Purple Finch
- ❏ Cassin's Finch
- ❏ *House Finch*
- ❏ Red Crossbill
- ❏ White-winged Crossbill
- ❏ Common Redpoll
- ❏ Hoary Redpoll
- ❏ Pine Siskin
- ❏ American Goldfinch
- ❏ Evening Grosbeak

**Old World Sparrows**
- ❏ House Sparrow

# Select References

American Ornithologists' Union. 1998. *Check-list of North American Birds.* 7th ed. (and its supplements). American Ornithologists' Union, Washington, D.C.

Butler, Elaine. 1991. *Attracting Birds.* Lone Pine Publishing, Edmonton, Alberta.

Elphick, C., J. B. Dunning, Jr., and D.A. Sibley, eds. 2001. *National Audubon Society The Sibley Guide to Bird Life & Behavior.* Alfred A. Knopf, New York.

Fisher, Chris, John Acorn. 1998. *Birds of Alberta.* Lone Pine Publishing, Edmonton, Alberta.

Roth, Sally. 1998. *Attracting Birds to Your Backyard 536 Ways to Turn Your Yard and Garden into a Haven for Your Favorite Birds.* Rodale Press, Inc. Emmaus, Pennsylvania.

Sibley, D. A. 2000. *National Audubon Society The Sibley Guide to Birds.* Alfred A. Knopf, New York.

# Index

Northern Saw-whet Owl